Inagawa Cemetery Chapel and Visitor Centre

猪名川霊園 礼拝堂・休憩棟

David Chipperfield Architects

デイヴィッド チッパーフィールド アーキテクツ

A place to pray and rest

In making a building for Inagawa Cemetery, we set out to create a place where anyone, regardless of religious or ethnic background, could pray, and a structure with the emotionally moving and calming qualities befitting the timelessness of a cemetery. David Chipperfield strongly endorsed the plan, and through our total and mutual respect for each other, we have attained the ultimate joy of collaborating as a 'trinity' of benefactor, architect and builder, without compromising in any way. These efforts have resulted in a splendid work of architecture that blends in perfectly with the surrounding landscape.

I see this chapel as a contemporary sanctuary that transcends religious denomination. Kind to visitors and a home to gods and Buddhas, without any particular religious affiliation, this is a place that allows us to rest. The building is unlike any other in the past, and as my friend, the artist Thomas Struth, aptly remarked, 'Small but big at the same time.' With its exquisite balance, it is also a place that is gentle yet strong, sacred yet intimate.

After the birth of the building, it is our job to cultivate its reason for being as those entrusted with the responsibility of raising it. As people from all over the world visit the site, it is our hope that the building will serve as a place of prayer that transcends religious and ethnic differences for generations to come, and that this philosophy will spread like ripples in the water.

Hideyuki Osawa
Chief Director of the Boenfukyukai Foundation

人が祈り、安らう場

猪名川霊園の建築を造るにあたってわたしたちがめざしたのは、宗教も人種も超えて誰もが分かち合える祈りの場と、墓地の永遠性にふさわしい感動と安らぎのある建築である。デイヴィッド・チッパーフィールド氏はこの構想に深く賛同してくれた。わたしたちが終始互いを尊重し、一切の妥協をせず、施主・設計者・施工者の「三位一体」となっての協働を成し遂げられたことは、このうえない喜びである。そしてその努力は、ランドスケープに見事に溶け込んだ素晴らしい建築として実を結んだ。

この礼拝堂はさながら、宗派を超えた現代の神殿のようだとわたしは感じている。人に優しく、どの宗教でもなく、神仏の住処でありながら、ひとが安らうことができる場所でもある。それは今まで見たこともない建物であり、いみじくも友人のアーティスト、トーマス・シュトルート氏が評したように、「小さいけれど大きい」のだ。そして絶妙なバランスで、それは「優しいけれど力強く」、「神聖だけれど親密」な場所なのである。

建築を生み落とした後、それを慈しみ育てる責任を担う者として、建物の存在価値をさらに発展させていくことが、わたしたちの使命だろう。そして世界中のひとびとが訪れてくれることで、幾世を経て、宗教も人種も超えて分かち合える祈りの場となり、その思想が波紋のように広がっていくことを願っている。

大澤秀行
公益財団法人墓園普及会理事長

Returning to Japan

The invitation to design this project gave me the opportunity to return to Japan 30 years after I first visited, and to work with the maturity of experience under very stimulating conditions—a sympathetic, committed and dedicated client, a beautiful location and a fascinating task. We also had the fortune to work with the most talented collaborators, and with skilled contractors and craftsmen. I am grateful for their professional experience but also for the cultural and personal experience they have given me.

This was an opportunity to pay homage to a culture that has inspired me throughout my career. Following my first visit to Japan in 1985, I had the good luck to study—through working here—the inherent values of Japanese design and aesthetic. It is an inspiration that has carried me through my professional life.

As I am writing this during a global pandemic, I'm wondering what could be more appropriate in our difficult times than to follow a careful celebration of the normal, to intensify through action and physical result the importance of things and their intrinsic qualities? Through the sensitive consideration of space, form, material, light and view, traditional Japanese architecture puts the individual at the centre. This is a humanistic and experiential idea—not a monumental one.

Architecture like all things is dependent on process as well as result. Although time dissolves the memory of process, it is embedded in the physical result. The success of any project depends on the spirit of its making. I believe that this project that we all made together carries and conveys the success and stimulation of a happy collaboration. I thank Hideyuki Osawa for the opportunity and Thomas Struth for introducing us in the knowledge that we would understand each other. I also thank Naoko Kawamura for coordinating the whole process, Matt Ball and our design team for developing the design, and Tom Herre for his dedication to following the project to the last detail. The project depends on the beautiful landscape design by Marcia Iwatate, and all of this was only possible through the collaboration with Key Operation Inc. Architects who realised the project with us. Finally, I am grateful to Obayashi Corporation and all the contractors, craftsmen and workers for their dedicated work and their impressive commitment to the quality of construction.

David Chipperfield
Principal of David Chipperfield Architects

日本に戻る

この猪名川霊園の設計を依頼されて、初訪日以来30年ぶりに日本に戻り、より深い経験を踏まえて、刺激に富む環境の下で仕事をすることができた。施主は思いやり深く、ひたむきかつ真摯、立地は美しく、つとめは魅力に富む。このプロジェクトに携わる間には、じつに才能豊かな協力者、技量に秀でた施工業者、そして職人の方々と共に仕事をする幸運にもめぐまれた。豊富な経験を生かしたプロジェクトへの貢献のみならず、そこで得られた文化的、私的な経験についても、みなさんに感謝したい。

今回のプロジェクトは、生涯を通じて建築家としてのわたしの歩みを触発してくれた文化に、謝意を表す機会ともなった。1985年に初めて来日してからというもの、この地で働くことによって、幸いにも日本の意匠、美意識に固有の価値を学ぶことができた。建築家としての日々の生業を支えてくれたのは、この間に得たインスピレーションにほかならない。

世界中に感染症が流行する今こうして執筆をしながら、この困難な時期には、用心しながらも当たり前のことを大切にし、行為と実際の成果を示すことによって、物事がほんらい具える美質を引き立てる以上に時宜に適うことはないのではないかと思う。空間、形態、素材、光、眺望を入念に考え抜くことにより、日本の伝統建築はひとりひとりの人間を重視した。これは経験を重んじ、人間を優先する考え方であり、こけおどしの大きさを求めない。

建築はすべての物事と同様に、過程が重要な役割を果たす。時間の経過によって過程の記憶は薄れるとはいえ、それは形を成して残る結果に深く根付く。プロジェクトがどのようなものであれ、その成否は完成に至るまでそれを支えた精神に左右される。わたしたち全員が力を合わせてなし遂げた今回のプロジェクトは、幸せな共同作業にともなう心の昂りと成果を保ち、伝えるにちがいない。プロジェクトに携わる機会を与えてくださった大澤秀行、互いに理解し合えるであろうと見抜き紹介の労をとってくれたトーマス・シュトルートに感謝したい。プロジェクト全体のまとめ役を担った川村直子、デザインの敷衍に携わったマット・ボールと我がデザイン・チーム、プロジェクトの最後のディテールの完遂まで全力をかたむけたトム・ヘーレの諸氏にもお礼を申し上げる。プロジェクトの成功は岩立マーシャの見事な造園設計に負うところ大であり、そのすべてはわたしたちと共にプロジェクトの実現を目指したキー・オペレーションの尽力抜きに不可能であったことはいうまでもない。最後に大林組、および各施工業者、職人、作業員のみなさんの献身的な働きと良質な物づくりに懸ける意気込みに感謝の意を捧げたい。

デイヴィッド・チッパーフィールド
デイヴィッド チッパーフィールド アーキテクツ代表

A note on the architecture

Inagawa Cemetery is located on a steep site in the Hokusetsu Mountain Range of the Hyogo prefecture, approximately 40 kilometres north of Osaka. The cemetery is laid out across terraces and bisected by a monumental flight of steps leading up to a shrine at the highest point—an axis that orients the whole project. The chapel and visitor centre is designed as a marked threshold between the outer world and a quieter space within for contemplation.

The programme is formally arranged under a single, sloping roof plane, following the view line from the entrance up to the shrine. The rooms of the visitor centre open onto the courtyard garden while the secluded chapel remains separate. An unadorned and quiet room with minimal heating and artificial lighting offers a non-denominational contemplative space, pure in its form. Relying on indirect sunlight from the gardens on either side, the chapel visitor finds seclusion and their focus is drawn to the essential rhythms of time through the natural indicators of daylight fluctuation and seasonal foliage changes.

On the diagonally opposite corner of the courtyard is the visitor centre. Two large rooms at the lower end of the roof provide for family gatherings and commemorations. The visitors lounge offers an informal area for resting and eating. The memorial room, which can be separated into three smaller rooms by pleated curtains made with *washi* paper on fabric, offers space for formal feasts after rituals.

The floors, walls and roof are formed as pure building elements and poured from the same earth-like red coloured concrete—honed for internal floors and ground and sandblasted for walkway walls and soffits—giving the overall structure a monolithic appearance. A range of furniture designed specifically for the project consisting of simple, informal painted wooden chairs, benches, tables can be re-arranged depending on the occasion.

Following the axial link between the two ends of the site, a rill carries water down the middle of the staircase from the top of the mountain directly towards the building. As it approaches the lower part of the staircase near the chapel, the running water slows and pools as it collects into a trough, then is diverted through a new underground channel under the site to the nearby canal.

David Chipperfield Architects

建築について

猪名川霊園は、大阪市から北へ約40キロに位置する、兵庫県は北摂山系の急斜面にある。ひな壇状に構成された霊園の中央を一本の階段がまっすぐに貫き、その頂点に納骨堂が立っている。この階段のラインこそは、建築の配置を決定づける軸線となった。

礼拝堂と休憩棟は、ここを訪れるひとびとを祈りのための静かな空間へと誘う場所として設計されている。山の中央階段の延長線上、納骨堂と反対の極をなす地点に、来園者の祈りと休憩のための空間を、中庭を取り囲むように配した。来園者は屋外のアプローチから、南東面中央の大きな開口部をくぐり、一段上がったこの空間に入る。

建物の構成としては、すべての機能を一枚の片流れの屋根の下に収め、そのラインが、エントランスから納骨堂を見上げたときの視線に沿うようにした。休憩棟の部屋はいずれも中庭に開かれている一方、礼拝堂だけは切り離されている。礼拝堂へは専用通路で外から直接入ることもでき、また、中庭から伸びるゆるやかな斜路を上がって到達することもできる。最小限の暖房と照明しかない、無垢で静謐なこの空間は、宗派を問わない純粋な祈りの場である。礼拝堂を訪れたひとびとにとっては、庭の両側から間接的に差し込む自然光が頼りとなり、ここで外界から遮断されるにつれ、刻々と変化する光や四季の移り変わりが刻む自然のリズムへと、感覚が研ぎ澄まされていく。庭はいずれも、日本の野山の色合いと質感を思い浮かべながら造ったもので、精選した種々の山野草や低木を緻密に配した。

中庭を挟んだ斜め向かいが休憩棟だ。低いほうの屋根の下に配したふたつの大きな部屋は、親族の集いや故人を偲ぶ場として使われる。ビジターラウンジは、気軽に休息をとったり、食事をしたりできる部屋である。メモリアルルームは、布に和紙を重ねた屏風式のカーテンで三つの部屋に仕切ることができ、そこでは法事の後の会食を行う。

建物は床も壁も屋根も、純粋な建築のエレメントとして形づくられている。いずれも赤土色に着色したコンクリートを素材とし、内部の床は磨き仕上げ、回廊の壁と軒下はサンドブラスト仕上げを施して、建物全体をひとつの岩の塊のように見せている。家具はすべてこの場所のために特別にデザインし、制作した。彩色を施したシンプルでカジュアルな木製の椅子、ベンチ、テーブルを、用途に応じて組み替えながら使うことができる。

敷地の両極を結ぶ軸線ともなっている急斜面の階段の真ん中を、山からの水が建物に向かって流れてくる。礼拝堂の脇に位置する階段の麓の部分に達すると水は速度をゆるめて水盤にいったん貯まり、そこから新しい地下水路に落ちて、すぐそばの小川へと流れ込むのだ。

デイヴィッド チッパーフィールド アーキテクツ

Photographs by Risaku Suzuki

写真　鈴木理策

Summer 夏

A conversation about places of prayer
David Chipperfield, Thomas Struth, Hideyuki Osawa

祈りの場をめぐる対話
デイヴィッド・チッパーフィールド×トーマス・シュトルート×大澤秀行

Photographs by Thomas Struth

写真　トーマス・シュトルート

特別の機会

トーマス・シュトルート［以下、TS］まず感じたのは、この霊園を撮影するのは難しい、ということ。それは悪いことではない。なにもかも写真に撮られなければいけないということはないからね。1時間か2時間ここにいたら、「デイヴィッドの人格が作品を通じて伝わってくるのがわかる」という気がした。

ほかの仕事と比べて、この建物を手がけたときにデイヴィッドは自分はいっそう自由だと感じたのではないか。

建物は山地の傾斜に沿い、横のひろがりを印象づける。縦長の墓石、山並みの上の空との対比が目立つ。建物は内気でも慎ましくもないけれども、だからといってでしゃばりはしない。敬意を払っている。与えられたものに目を向けて、そこにあるものを見つめ、できることのほうに進み、どうすれば力になれるかと考える。

建物のディテールは洗練を究め、繊細なドローイングを思わせる。霊園のパンフレットを見たときに、漢字の使い方に興味を覚えた。ラテン語の手書きの文字と似ている。ここで使われる漢字は親や先祖、あるいは友人のようにごく親しいひとを亡くしたときにひとの感じる、人間しか知り得ない経験にそぐうように工夫されている。それはあらかじめ用意された些細な気遣いのひとつにすぎないとしても、やはり心を動かされる。

周囲の景観がこの建物の核をなしている。日本の庭園や寺院を訪れると、人間の手で造られた庭園を自然に娶らせようとしているとわかるけれども、典型的なイギリス式やフランス式庭園はそれとは正反対だ。日本人は和もう、娶ろうとする。岩や石は人工的に並べられたようにはみえず、たまたまそこにあるように見える。それは心のなかの想像力から生まれながら、心象は水のように流れて、すぐに手許をすりぬける。

この建物も、そうした庭園と同じように、実際にここに来て経験するのがよい。とっくりと見るように、ひとに誘いかける。

A special opportunity

TS My first impression was that the cemetery was difficult to photograph. That is not a bad thing. Not everything needs to be photographed. After spending an hour or two here, I thought, 'Oh, I can sense David's personality coming through in the work'.

I suspect that David felt freer with this building than he did with other works.

The building follows the sloping mountain line and highlights the horizontal—a contrast to the vertical gravestones and the sky above the mountainous landscape. It is not a shy or modest building, yet it is also not intrusive; it strikes a respectful tone. You look at the given, see what exists, and steer toward what could be possible, how you can contribute.

The details of the building are extremely refined and make one think of a delicate drawing. When I saw the cemetery leaflet, I thought the way the Japanese characters are used was interesting. They are similar to the qualities of Latin script, handwriting. The characters were crafted for the specifically human experience that people have when someone close—a parent, ancestor, or friend—dies. It is only another detail, but nonetheless moving.

The public landscape is at the heart of the building. When you go to Japanese gardens or temples, you see attempts to marry wild nature with the man-made garden, whereas with typical English or French gardens, it is the complete opposite. The Japanese want to make peace, to marry things together. Rocks do not look artificially arranged but rather as if they just happen to be there. It has to do with the imagination of the inner mind, but inner images are fluid—they escape quickly.

This, like those gardens, is a place that you have to come to in order to experience. It seduces you to look at it.

DC Japanese architecture, which inspired this project, is traditionally wooden. The work is less tectonic and more constructive, so there is a paradox: the structure bears the influence of that legacy, but it also has a kind of monolithic presence.

Aside from the duality of the aesthetics, the framework I worked in was another key part of the process. The professional context of this project allowed me to work in a more personal way. I drew all the sketches and supervised the models; it was like going back to my early days. Thomas, however successful he gets, still has to press the button on his camera. He still directs; he still frames everything. If you are an architect, things are different. As your practice gets bigger and there are more projects, you become more distanced from some of the smaller decisions.

With this project, however, I was back to designing and directing the process in a close way, which was very nice. At first, I was scared of the project because it is far from home, small in scale, and it was a very personal decision to do it—it called out to my long-standing enthusiasm for Japan.

But being scared added value to the experimentation, and the scale allowed me to reconnect to many aspects of the project simultaneously. Bigger projects have bigger issues and bigger budgets. As soon as you have a huge budget,

デイヴィッド・チッパーフィールド［以下、DC］今回のプロジェクトの発想の源にもなった日本の伝統建築は、木で造られる。この建物は形成的であるよりも構成的だから、パラドックスがある。建物の構造はそうした遺産の影響を残しながら、一枚岩のような存在感もあわせもつ。

美意識のこうした二重性は別にして、作業のしかたにも今回の仕事では重要な意味があった。プロジェクトへの関わり方に特徴があり、いつもより自分で手を下せる場面が多かった。スケッチはすべて自分で描いたし、模型の制作にも目を配った。昔に戻ったみたいだったよ。トーマスの場合には、どれほど成功を収めたところで、カメラのボタンは押さなければならない。今でも演出の指示を出す。すべてのフレーミングはまだ本人がする。建築家となると、そうはいかない。仕事の規模が大きくなって、あつかうプロジェクトの数が増えれば、重要性の低い判断のなかには、自分の手を離れてゆくものも出てくる。

それが今回のプロジェクトでは、自分の手の届くところでデザインをし、指示を出す以前のやり方に戻ることができて、それがとても心地よかった。初めのうち、このプロジェクトには怖じ気づいてね。本拠地から遠いし、規模は小さいし、引き受けることにしたのは、きわめて個人的な理由からだった。昔からの日本贔屓に訴えかけるところがあったものでね。

しかし怖じ気づいたからこそ、この試みの価値が高まったし、規模が小さいためにプロジェクトの様々な側面に同時並行的に目を配ることができた。プロジェクトが大きければ問題も大きいし、予算も大きくなる。予算が巨大になれば、多くの危険をともなう。危険が増えれば、20人が集って決定を下すようになる。ひとりが決めるのではなくてね。

今回の施主はただひとり、それも素晴らしいひとだ。すべての決定は秀さん（大澤秀行氏のこと）が下す。そうしたありかたは住宅ならよくあるけれども、住宅は規模がごく私的な範囲にとどまる。猪名川霊園のプロジェクトはじつに素晴らしかった。それは個人住宅でないにもかかわらず、ごく私的なレベルで決定が下されるからだ。

秀さんは辛抱強い。第一段階は、秀さんがわたしに何をしてもらいたいのか理解することだった。

当初、それが「何か」は理解した。ところがそれがどのようなものでありうるかは、どうしても理解できなかった。

デザインという作業は、あのものが何になりたがっているかを理解することだね。どんどん掘り下げて、その主体が機能、目的、ものとしてのありかたなどの面で、どのようなものになりたいかを理解しようと努める。これらの質問にすべて応えるのは並大抵のことではない。

もちろん、そこにはもうひとつやっかいな問題がある。デザインに関して高度に洗練された感受性をもち、輪郭の明確な文化のなかに外国人として身を置いて仕事をすれば、避けがたく生じる文化の受け渡しをどうするかという問題だ。わたしは日本文化を敬してやまないし、それがために作業はいっそう難しくなる。わたしは全生涯をつうじて日本文化の影響を受けてきたし、世界中のプロジェクトにそれを採り入れようとする試みをつづけてきた。日本国内で異国人として働く場合に、自分のデザインが日本的と受けとめられたいと願うことはまずなさそうだが、何にしても日本で意味をもつためには、少なくとも日本的な美意識に配慮しなければならない。

わたしは日本でこれまでに30年仕事をしてきた。初めのうちは、自分の背景がどういうものか知らなかった。日本で手がけたいくつかのプロジェクトは、わたしが初めて設計した建物でもあったから、自分自身の自伝のページを繰っていたことになる。イギリスの建築家が日本でイギリスの建物を造っているのか、それとも日本建築を真似ているのかについても、ほとんど何も考えていなかった。この頃はかならずしもそうならなくてもすむ。秀さんも言うように、肚でわかることなんだな。自分の直感を信じて、背景にある事情の表裏を巧みに往来する必要はなくなった。

トーマスが風景の借用について話したね。借用という考え方はわたしにとってもきわめて重要だ。どのプロジェクトにもそれを埋めこもうとしているものでね。今日の建築のほとんどはある場所に運ばれてゆき、そこにぽんと置かれる。いずれにしろ、その場に埋めこまれはしない。わたしはひとが前に見たことがあると感じながら、そうと意識しなかったものを作りた

there are lots of risks. As soon as there are lots of risks, twenty people are making decisions—not one person.

In this case, we had just one client—an extraordinary one. Hide-san (Hideyuki Osawa) made every decision. That pattern is common in projects like houses, but houses are very personal in scope. The Inagawa Cemetery project was great because it was not a private domestic building but it was still decided in a very personal manner.

Hide-san was patient. The first step was to understand what he was asking me to do. At the beginning, I understood *what* it was—but I did not quite understand what it *could* be.

Designing is the act of understanding what something wants to be. You just dig and dig, trying to understand what the subject wants to be in terms of function, purpose, and physical nature. Answering all those questions well was a challenge.

Of course, there was another complexity: the cultural transfer inherent in working as a foreigner in a highly articulated culture with a sophisticated design sensibility. I have enormous respect for Japanese culture, which makes the task even more difficult. The Japanese design culture has influenced me my whole life, and I have tried to bring it into projects around the world. Working as an outsider within Japan, you do not necessarily want your design to appear Japanese—but for things to have meaning in Japan, you have to at least be conscious of the Japanese aesthetic.

I have been working in Japan for 30 years. At first, I did not know what my context was. The first projects here were my first buildings, so I was discovering my own autobiography. I also had little idea of whether I was an English architect in Japan doing an English building or one trying to imitate Japanese architecture. Nowadays, it does not have to be like that. As Hide-san says, it is a gut thing. I can just trust my instincts without having to navigate between the two sides of the context.

Thomas talked about borrowing the landscape. The idea of borrowing is vital to me because I try to embed that into each project. Most architecture now is landed into a place, after all, not embedded. I am interested in creating something that *has* been seen before but not actually seen on a conscious level. I would like people to find a project familiar and knowable, even when seeing it for the first time.

Beyond physicality

HO To me, architecture is not so much about form or details but more about what people feel when they step into it. A project would be a failure if visitors could not feel what we felt or be moved like we were moved.

That was the mindset I took into the last project, *Sayama Lakeside Cemetery* (2013), which was designed by a young Japanese architect named Hiroshi Nakamura (Hiroshi Nakamura & NAP). In that effort, it was immensely rewarding to see how my vision could translate into actual form. This second project was with you, David Chipperfield, and you come from a European background.

いと考えている。初めて見るのに、これには馴染みがある、これならわかると感じてもらいたい。

形あるものを超えて

大澤秀行［以下、HO］　建築で最も大切なことは、形式やディテールの美しさなどの細かいことではなく、訪れるひとがその建物に入ったときにまず何を感じるか、ということだ。訪れたひとがそこでわたしたちが感じたのと同じように感じ、心を動かされるのでなかったら、プロジェクトとして成功したとは言えないだろう。

そんなことを考えて手がけたのが、日本人の若手建築家・中村拓志さん（中村拓志＆NAP建築設計事務所）が設計したひとつ前のプロジェクトの《狭山湖畔霊園》（2013）だ。これで自分のヴィジョンを形にできた手ごたえを得た。そしてつぎに、ヨーロッパの建築家であるデイヴィッド・チッパーフィールド、君とやった。今回はある意味で自分にとってのチャレンジだったよ。例えば言葉の問題。英語でのコミュニケーションでは、わたしが思っていることの十分の一も伝えられない気がして、ミーティングのたびに悔しい思いがあったからね。しかしデイヴィッドは、非常に大きな心で胸襟を開いて向き合ってくれた。幾度もやりとりを重ねるなかで理解を深めていってくれた。

《猪名川霊園》オープンの前夜祭の会場となった両足院（建仁寺塔頭）の副住職・伊藤東凌さんが霊園へいらしたとき、「この非常にミニマルな空間からは、禅の精神を感じる」とおっしゃった。そこでわたしは彼に説明した。デイヴィッドが日本で初めて仕事をしてから30年というあいだ、彼は、日本の文化を尊敬し、愛し、味わってきた。それが彼の身体のなかで長い時間をかけて消化され、表現ににじみ出てきた。ステレオタイプの日本のイメージを表面的になぞったのではない。そのようなデイヴィッドだからこそ、言語を超えてわたしの意味するところを理解してもらえた。

トーマスとわたしには、長い時間で培ってきた、よい刺激を与え合える関係があった。そして、デイヴィッドとも、彼のその素養のおかげで、同じように刺激を与え合える関係を築けた。それがこの建物や場所に対するお互いの考えを理解し合うことに大きく影響を与えたはずだ。その結果、素晴らしい建築、いや、建築を超えて、素晴らしい場を造ったと言えるんじゃないかと思っている。

DC　わたしも建築とは場を造ることだと思う、それはまちがいない。建築にはじつに多くの、様々な責任があり、潜在的な可能性もある。まずは、ものとして。床、壁、小屋を造れる。小屋に穴をあけ、ひとを外にさらして、外と結びつけることによって、穴に関係性をもたせる機会を得る。ダイナミックなこの関わりを自在にあやつれるようになれば、じつにおもしろいことが起こりうる。

それとはまた別に、建築にはものを超えたひろがりがある。物事を秩序立てる力があり、社会と関わる潜在的な力がある。

建築家というものは、このふたつの潜在性の間を渡り歩くわけだね。このふたつを結びつけなければいけないとわたしは思う。ものとしてしっかり存在するもの、ものらしいものを作らなければ、わたしたちの技能は無駄に費やされてしまう。しかしものとしての存在が主題であってはならない。建築は主題を表現することばなのだから。猪名川霊園の建物の主題は物質ではなく、もっと深い、ひとびとを励ます力なのだろう。ものとしての存在は、思想をたしかなものにする。思想はものとしての側面がないと、あやふやで脆くなる。しかしディテールそのものが興味深いということはない。建築家が知りたいのは「何が」ではなく「どのようにして」、それから「なぜ」だからね。秀さんはよくわたしに「デイヴィッド、きみはディテールのあつかいがじつに上手い」と言った。ところが、わたしのほうはディテールには少しも興味がない。興味がもてるのは、思想が宿る場合にかぎられる。そこから概念の表現につながる広い道が拓ける。プロジェクトの要旨は思想なんだ。しかしものとしての存在抜きに思想を創り出すことはできない。建築の大半はその道半ばで迷子になって、できあがった建物の一部は理知の思想、一部は社会の思想、一部はものとしての思想にとどまる。

To me, it was a challenge because I could hardly express any of what I was thinking. I was always frustrated in meetings, wishing I were able to say more than I could. But David was so receptive and open-minded that it was never really an issue. As we talked, we understood each other better.

Toryo Ito, a Zen Buddhist priest from Ryosoku-in, Kenninji Temple, where we held a traditional ritual the night before the opening of the cemetery, came here and said he felt this space was truly minimal, that he sensed the spirit of Zen. I told him that David has respected, loved, and enjoyed Japanese culture for the past 30 years—he had probably digested his whole experience on a deep level, almost bodily, and the experience had just come out naturally or subconsciously in the architecture. It was not just a superficial rendering of a Japanese aesthetic stereotype.

Since David has that background and sensitive capacity for understanding, I think my thoughts got through to him—even past my language shortcomings. Thomas and I have built a rewarding, stimulating relationship over all these years. David and I have a certain chemistry, too, just like Thomas and I do. David's sensibilities are so refined that it was easy to connect with him on an exciting level—we can play off each other. That was the key to our mutual understanding, which was so crucial to bringing the architecture here—no, the place here—such a wonderful fruition.

DC I think architecture is about making place, definitely. Architecture has so many different responsibilities and potentialities, too. The first is the physical. You can make a floor, a wall, a shelter. Then you have an opportunity to make a hole in the shelter, and have the hole create a relationship, exposing and connecting you to the outside. Once you start playing with that dynamic, it can be fascinating.

On the other hand, architecture goes beyond the physical. It has an organising power, the potentiality to be societal.

As architects, we jump between these two potentialities. I believe that you have to combine both. Our skills go to waste unless we make things that have physical qualities, a kind of thingness. The physicality, though, should not be the subject—it is the words that express the subject. The subject of the Inagawa Cemetery building is not the material but rather the deeper, empowering quality. Physicality reassures the idea; the idea is less assured, more fragile, if it has no substantial dimension. But a detail is not interesting on its own. Architects want to know the how and the why, not the what. Hide-san would say to me, 'Ah, David, you are so good at detail'. I am not the slightest bit interested in detail, though! Only in that it allows for an idea; it opens avenues for a concept to come through. The idea is the thrust of the project, but you cannot make the idea without also having the substance. Most architecture gets lost in the middle, where the works is partly an intellectual idea, partly a societal idea, and partly a physical idea.

Hide-san created an environment where we could experiment with both of these issues: what this place could

秀さんはわたしたちがそうしたふたつの問題について実験することのできる環境を創り出してくれた。ものとしてこの場は何か、ということも重要だが、もうひとつ社会の視点、あるいはここに墓参りに来るひとびとの視点から見て、この場のもつ意味は何か。秀さんは建築家がそうした問題と心置きなく取り組める機会を提供してくれた。施主のなかには、そのような社会的な問題に関心のないひとも少なくない。施主はただ建物のデザインを求めて、建築家に金を払う。秀さんはどんなものであれ、その意味の潜在力を知りたがるという点でユニークだね。

TS　わたしもそう思う。それが秀の出発点だったし、初めて話を聞いて、途方もないプロジェクトだと思ったのはそのせいだった。これをより広い意味の建築にあてはめることもできるだろう。愛するひとを亡くし悼む厳かな営みを行う場をよりよくデザインするのに、並外れた洞察力と感受性が求められることは言うまでもない。

建築が実現するまでの過程で、実際に必要とされているのは何か、完成したものはどのように使われるかを見つめる時間が充分でないことがよくあるような気がする。

文化への問い

DC　つまり、必要から出発して、それ以上のものに導くにはどうすればよいか。問題はそこにある。施主の大半は建物を必要とする、営利目的か、あるいは実用的な面から何かを必要としている。我々はそのうえにもうひとつ別の志向を重ねる、そこから始めて、それ以上にできることがあると考えてのことだね。

TS　まさにその通り。とはいえ解決法に欠陥があると、できあがった建物はのべつ対立をあげつらうことになる。建物は「無知と傲慢」くらいにしか見えない。

DC　必要と志向は写真にもあてはまる。我々は写真というもの自体は必要としないかもしれないが、ある意味で必要性はある。写真はまずなによりも手軽だ。しかしその手軽さの先に目を向けると、何かの内側に意味をこめるために写真を用いる必要性に思い至る。

TS　それは芸術の問題だろう。つまりだね、芸術とは経験を芸術作品に作り替えることだ。

DC　それでは、なぜ写真はどこかの地点でたんなる写真ではなく芸術作品になるのだろう。

TS　もし必要に迫られていないとすると、そもそもなぜ写真を撮るかという理由に左右される。例えば、今朝きみの設計した建物を撮影したときに、写真家になりたての頃、建築家やアーティストのために写真を撮らなければならなかったことを思い出した。あれはどうしても好きになれなかった、なぜかというと……。

DC　頼まれ仕事だからかな。

TS　頼まれ仕事のなかには、ひどくつまらないものもあったよ。

DC　我々は依頼を受けて初めて仕事する。発端はきわめて明確、責任の所在と成果物を明確に定めた契約がある。

TS　そうだね、しかし写真はそうではない。だれもがわたしの写真を見なければならないということはないが、建物は実際に存在する。公共の場に長い間、存在しつづける。

DC　写真家として、きみは自分の作品を自ら決定することができる。写真はほかに頼らず、そのもの自体で完結する。なぜなら、きみはひとの手を借りずにその写真を作れるからだ。建築家である我々は、つねに他者を介して仕事をする。今回のプロジェクトでは、集団的知性のもつ意味合いが心に響い

be physically, which is important, but also what it could be in terms of meaning, from the perspectives of society and the people who come here to pay their respects. He created an opportunity where an architect could comfortably experiment with these things. Often, clients are not interested in these societal issues; they pay you just to design a building. Hide-san is unique in that he wants to know the potentiality in the meaning of everything.

TS I agree. That was Hide's starting point—and why I thought the project was so incredible when he initially told me about it. You could even extrapolate this to architecture in a broader sense. Of course, designing a better environment for the difficult situation of commemorating lost loved ones requires a particular acknowledgement and sensitivity.

I think in an architectural process, there is often not enough time to carefully look at what is actually needed and what the result will be for.

A question of culture

DC So, how can we lead a necessity into becoming something more? That is the issue. Most clients are motivated by necessity, needing something commercially or practically. Then we lay another aspiration on top, thinking we can do more from it.

TS Exactly! But if the solution is flawed, the resulting architecture speaks all the time about conflict. The building is there to say 'ignorance, arrogance' and so forth.

DC The ideas of necessity and aspiration apply to photography, too. We might not *need* photography as such, but there is a necessity in one sense. Photography is eminently accessible. But looking past that accessibility, the need is to use photography to put meaning *inside* something.

TS That is a question of art. I mean, art is the transformation of an experience into a work of art.

DC So why does a photograph at some point become a work of art as opposed to just a photograph?

TS It depends on why you make the photograph in the first place, if it has no immediate purpose. For example, when I photographed your building this morning, I was reminded of how, early in my career, I had to make photographs for architects and artists. It was something I never liked because…

DC Because of the commissions?

TS Some commissions were pretty boring!

DC We only operate on commission, with a very clear beginning, a very clear contract of responsibility and the deliverable.

TS Yes, but photography is different. Nobody has to look at my pictures, but a building really exists; it has a lasting presence in the public realm.

DC As a photographer, you can define your work yourself. It has its own autonomous integrity because you can make it independently. As architects, we can only work through others. The sense of group intelligence really resonated with me during this project. Look at the graphics on the wall. The graphics are very beautiful,

た。壁に掛かるあのサインを見てごらん。とても美しいけれども、あそこに至るまでにはサインより文化について論ずることのほうがずっと多かった。

TS　どういうふうに？

DC　漢字と英語が必要かどうかを決めなければならない。まず、サインが必要と気づく。建物にサインや案内を添えるのは技術的な問題のはずなのに、それが文化的な見方に照らして、じつに興味深いものになった。そこで新しい疑問が生じる。なぜここに英語が必要か。ここに来て英語の文字を必要とするのは、どんなひとなのか。

TS　そんなひとはいない。ここに家族が埋葬されている外国人がいるとは思えない。

DC　そうだろう。わたしはなぜここに英語を添えなければいけなのか、と理由を問わずにいられなかった。それに見かけもよくない。デザインを考え、文字が美しく見えるようにするために、ほんとうに長い時間をかけた。つまるところ、これはデザインの問題ではなかった。わたしたちは意味、文化、詩情について論じ合った。最も手軽なのは英語と漢字を使うことで、そうすればだれも傷つかない。しかし一歩下がって、自問しないわけにいかないだろう。なぜ最も手軽な解決法を採るのかと。

ほとんどのプロジェクトでは、委員会があり、すべての決定を下すから、結局のところあれやこれやの国の言語がリストに加わることになる。ところがこのプロジェクトの施主は、たったひとりだ。問いただし、話し合う相手は、ひとりの人間なんだよ。だから何にしてもずっと刺激的で、精緻で、より人間的になる。

TS　結果として、とても小さな、目立たないものになった。多様な楽器のなかからいちばん地味な音色を選んだと言えるかな、ある意味ではね。

DC　自分では、実用性を高めて、標識を目障りなものからプロジェクトの精神を強めるものに変えたと思う。これはほうっておいて、自然にそうなるものではない。対話から、長い時間をかけ、ときにはかなり熱のこもった対話を繰り返した末に得られたものだ。

TS　それによって準備の過程、意思疎通の際の焦点がより絞られ、よりよい結果が得られた。

DC　そうだね、たいがいのプロジェクトでは、それほど激しい議論と出合うことはめったにない。普通なら、わたしにしても秀さんにしても、そうした話し合いに加わることさえなかったろう。それでも慎重に事を運ぶ必要がある、当然ながらね。考えもなく仕事にかかって、案内板をあまりなまくらにしてしまえば、できあがるのは酷いデザインだ。我々は三度ここに立って、サインについて話し合った。まず寸法、デザインについて話した。わたしの考えるに、作業はデザインのみに関わるのではなく、重要なのは何を言おうとするのか、サインはなんのために必要か、ということだ。

HO　それは文化の違いよりも、まず人間性の違いだろう。そのひとの意識レベルが低いと、問題の捉え方の次元がちがうから、うまくコミュニケーションできない。文化を共有しているはずの日本の建築家とでさえうまくいかないことがある。文化の違いというのは、じつは大した問題ではない。それよりもまず、ひととしてどのような意識をもっているのかがいちばん大きな問題だ。そこからのコミュニケーションがうまくいかなくては、一緒にものを作っていくことは難しい。

その点、デイヴィッドは素晴らしかった。ある対象に対して、本質は何かということを常に考えているひとで、コミュニケーションがすごく取りやすかった。わたし自身も慣例に倣うのではなく、なぜそうするべきなのかを常に考えているタイプだから。そこを共有できるという信頼感がこのプロジェクトの根底にあった。彼が日本の文化を自分の一部であるかのように理解していることもあり、文化の違いはまったく問題にならなかった。ただし、ウォシュレットを理解してもらうのはなかなか大変だったけれどね！（笑）

but the journey to that point was less about a discussion of graphics and more about a discussion of culture.

TS In what way?

DC You have to establish whether you need the kanji and the English. First, you realise you need a sign. Adding graphics and signage to a building is a technical issue, which then turns out to be quite interesting from a cultural perspective. You arrive at new questions. Why do we need English here? Who is going to come and need the English letters?

TS Nobody. What foreigner would have a family member buried here?

DC Right. I had to ask why they were adding English, as it did not look nice. We spent so much time making the design and ensuring that the letters would look beautiful. In the end, it was not a design problem—it was a discussion of meaning and culture and poetics. The easiest thing is to put English and kanji; it would not harm anyone. But you have to step back and ask yourself: why should we just take the easiest solution?

For most projects, there would be a committee to make all the decisions, and you could potentially end up with all sorts of languages added to the list. But this project had a single client—just one person to interrogate and discuss things with—so it all became more stimulating, precise, and more human.

TS The result is quite small and subdued. It comes through like the lowest tone of an instrumental palette, in a way.

DC In my eyes, we turned the graphics from an inconvenience into something that strengthens the spirit of the project, enhancing the practical programme. That does not just happen. It comes from dialogue, a prolonged—and sometimes contentious—series of discussions.

TS Which give the process, the whole protocol of communication, a sharper focus and better results.

DC Yes. In most projects, you rarely encounter discussions that intense; under normal circumstances, neither I nor Hide-san would probably have even been involved in the talks. You still need to exercise caution, of course. If you do something without thinking and make the signage too obtuse, then you end up with a bad design. We stood here three times to discuss the graphics. At the beginning, it was about size, about design. In my opinion, the process is not about the design alone—the important things are what you are trying to say and what you need the signage for.

HO Finding a common ground is a process with many layers. It is much more about differences in awareness than about differences in culture. It depends on the nature of the person; if the awareness is low, the level of the issues that come up is low, and that frustrates communication. Even with a Japanese architect—with no cultural gap in play—a difference in awareness would make it difficult to communicate. Compared to cultural gaps, the bigger deciding factor is awareness compatibility: how you think and whether you look at things on a fundamental level. Without that shared awareness, it would be difficult to make things together even if both parties were Japanese.

But David was superb in terms of awareness. He always approached things from the fundamental level. It was easy

施主の哲学

TS　秀とは長い付き合いになる。東京の島田画廊で展覧会をしていた頃に、わたしの作品を蒐集してくれて、親しくなり、今では互いに「兄弟」と呼び合っている。秀とは話しやすい、それはアメリカで教育を受けたからかもしれない。あるときニューヨークで偶然行きあうことがあって、秀から建築に興味をもち始めたこと、それから財団の霊園にある建物の雰囲気を改善したいという話を聞いた。愛するひとの灰を埋葬しに訪れる方々に、より荘厳な経験をしてもらえるようにしたいと言う。その話に心を動かされた。人間の経験を分析して、それをある種の建築的な表現に結びつけたいと願うひとがいるということに。それには、原則として、経験の共有が前提になるだろう。当初、秀は日本人の建築家を起用することしか考えていなかった。

デイヴィッドとはその2、3年前にベルリンで出会い、日本を愛していると知っていた。デイヴィッドにわたしの日本人の友人の考えを伝え、秀にはデイヴィッドが2012年のヴェネチア・ビエンナーレ国際建築展の総合ディレクターを務めるヴェネチアに来れば紹介するからともちかけることができて、わたしは嬉しく思う。友だちといろいろな話をして、たがいにアイデアをもちだしては盛り上がることがよくあるだろう。たいがいは、もちろんそれっきりで終わってしまう。今回は、それが実を結んだ。うまくいきそうな予感はしたよ。とにかく、これがそもそもの始まりだった。

DC　コレクターとして、秀さんは芸術家の感受性と付き合う辛抱強さがある。芸術家はあつかいづらく、こだわりの強いひとも多い。優れた建築家と共に仕事をする件については、秀さんにはすでに……。

TS　忍耐力がある。

DC　……。忍耐力か（笑）。建築家の話を聞くということに関して、秀さんはとても寛容で、相手を尊重してくれる。アングロサクソン文化では、建築家は役務提供者と見なされることが多い。建築家に期待されるのは文化に関する洞察ではなく、プロとしての仕事、業務の履行、イメージ、それからうまくいけばちょっとした宣伝効果といったところだね。そうした文化を背景にして、建築家という職業は珍しい地位を占める。

我々は芸術家を奇妙な動物とみなす。我々に代わって新しいアイデアを思いつき、文化を探求してくれるひとというわけだ。ところが建築家はその範疇に収まらない。建築家は堅実な、現実世界に属する。しかしアングロサクソン文化とはちがって、日本文化は建築家の役割をきわめて高く評価する。

我々の文化が市場に主導されたものであることを考えれば、建築家が役務提供者であるのは言うまでもない。建築家はそのように思考しなければならないし、そのためにいささか追従しがちにもなる。どうすればあまり気難しいと思われずにすむかを学ぶ。気難しいと、プロジェクトが逃げていく。我々は施主の意見に耳を傾ける。施主が「ここはどうすればよいか、わからない」と言うと、我々はつい「もちろん、そうでしょう。あなたは正しい」と応えてしまう。これは変えてもいい。優れた施主——秀は非常に優れた施主だ——は我々に「わたしも、わかりません」と答えてほしいのだと思う。これを受けいれる感受性があり、それが日本人の感受性なのではないだろうか。

HO　わたしには哲学がある。素晴らしい建築を造るには、「三位一体」が非常に大切だということ。今回も、まず施主と建築家のふたりが互いに尊敬し合いながら議論を重ねて理解を深め合った。それは建設業者にも伝わり、三者が思いを分かち合いながら、同じゴールに向かっていった。悔いのない人生を送ることが、わたしの人生のモットーだが、この建築プロジェクトもそのひとつだった。妥協することなくデイヴィッドと徹底的にやれたことがとても幸せだった。自分の人生のモットーを貫徹したことで、素晴らしい場を造ることに成功したんだと思う。

to communicate with him, in that sense. I try to avoid blindly going with the customary practices; I always think about *why* it should be that way. David and I are a lot alike in that sense. Knowing that we were both on the same page created a sense of trust between us, which was vital to the project. David seems to understand Japanese culture like it makes up a part of who he is, so it was effortlessly easy to bridge any cultural differences. The only real challenge I had was explaining and reaching an agreement on the Washlet—a toilet seat with automated bidet features!

The client's philosophy

TS Hide and I have known each other for a long time. During the time I showed with Gallery Shimada in Tokyo, he collected my work and we started to become friends—'brothers', as we now call each other. I always find him easy to talk to, maybe because of his education in the United States. One day when we met in New York, he told me about his new interest in architecture, and his intention to improve the atmosphere of the building structures at the cemeteries of his foundation. He wanted to create a more dignified experience for the people who come to bury the ashes of their loved ones. I found it very touching, that someone would want to let the analysis of a human experience lead to a particular architectural expression. This is, in principle, about a shared experience. Initially, he wanted to work with Japanese architects only.

David and I had met a few years earlier in Berlin, and I knew about his love for Japan. It was a pleasure telling David about my Japanese friend's idea and suggesting that Hide come to Venice when David curated the Architecture Biennale in 2012 so that they could meet. We often discuss things with friends and get excited floating ideas to each other. Most of the time, of course, nothing comes of it. In this case, though, something did happen. I had an insight that it could work out. Whatever it was, that was all it took.

DC As a collector, Hide-san has a tolerance for an artist's sensibilities. He is used to artists. Artists are difficult, often very particular. When it comes to collaborating with a good architect, he already has…

TS Patience.

DC …Patience, yes! [*Laughs*] He was very generous and respectful to the idea of listening to the architect. In Anglo-Saxon culture, the architect tends to be a service provider. Instead of expecting cultural insight from an architect, you want professional service, performance, image, and hopefully a little bit of promotion. In that cultural context, the profession occupies an unusual position.

We see artists as strange animals, thinking on our behalf of new ideas and investigating culture, but architects do not fall into that category of perception. They are part of the hard, real world. But unlike the Anglo-Saxon culture, Japanese culture still holds the role of the architect in very high regard.

Architects are service providers, of course, given our market-driven culture. Architects have to think that way and, therefore, they also become a little bit obsequious. We learn not to be too difficult; if you are difficult, you lose the project. We listen to the client. The client says, 'I'm not sure about this', and we often say, 'Of course. You are right'. We could change that. I think good clients—and Hide is a very good client—want us to say, 'I'm not sure, either'. There is a sensibility about this, a Japanese sensibility.

HO I have a basic philosophy: a wonderful piece of architecture hinges on a trinity of spirit. First, the client and the architect have to respect each other so that they can discuss anything to reach a solution, which the builder then shares in. The three parties share the same goal, passion, and feelings.

My motto is to live life with no regrets. That applies to this architectural project as well. I am so happy that David and I could pursue this project with no compromises and no regrets. I felt like embracing and following that motto is what made this wonderful place a reality.

At the stopping point

中継地にて

Toshiyuki Horie

堀江敏幸

There is a quiet glow to buildings on hillsides and mountainsides. What really pull me in are the structures which intentionally superimpose geometric beauty over the backdrop of the sloped land, rather than trying to immerse themselves in the surrounding topography—they have a visual exteriority which accentuates the little mathematical miracles pervading nature. Whenever I am at one, I find myself wondering whether I should be looking down at everything from above or gazing up from below.

⁎

On a steep slope in Hyogo's Hokusetsu Mountain Range sits Inagawa Cemetery. The centrepiece of the space is a chapel with a mono-pitched roof slanting down toward some unseen sea, a visual effect similar to that of the Sea Ranch condominium overlooking the Pacific Ocean. It is not the first slope-based cemetery I have ever been to. There is Père Lachaise Cemetery in Paris, for example, where the geometry of the place is a meticulously calculated chaos. The boughs of planted trees in artificial plots hang over the walking paths, clad in the hues and shapes of nature, imbuing the space with deep shadows and quietude. Energy flows at will, unimpeded. Instead of letting silence come over the space, the cemetery actively creates dialogues with the dead; questions find answers. But the administration building, where personnel keep watch over the space, strikes an odd chord with the land, the structure's dull, monotonous tones sticking out like a suburban house in a forest.

⁎

At Inagawa Cemetery, however, there are only questions. There is no sense of imposition, nothing forcing the dead to respond. Look at Suzuki Risaku's photographs of the place, snapshots of the cemetery in its seasonal cycle, and you see a monologue—nothing but questions, inquiries expecting no answer in return. Knowing that you are the only one who can hear your inner voice deepens the experience; a question with no hope for an answer is that much more searching, that much more resonant. Cemeteries are places where individual people reside after death, of course, but Inagawa Cemetery does not exude that personal specificity. It is a lot like a public cemetery, one where anonymity pervades the space, creating blank mental canvases which give visitors' imaginations more freedom to roam and ruminate. Yes, the cemetery preserves a sense of ownership; the memories can be mine, yours, my father's, my mother's, my husband's, my wife's, my son's, my daughter's. The possessive nature of death and grief is there, but it is not front and centre. The place strips death down to its purest form. David Chipperfield did not *design* the cemetery. He just paid his respects to the death there, the product of years and years of natural progression, faithfully excavating the vibrant reality of death out from under layers of time like an archaeologist bringing the ruins of Pompeii out from shrouds of volcanic ash. Chipperfield knows how anonymity and innocuousness do not always have to translate into a cold, distant impersonality.

⁎

The dynamics of closedness and openness mingle in harmony at Inagawa Cemetery. Evoking the simplicity of a Romanesque church and the look of classic wooden architecture in ruddy colours, avoiding white hues, the design wraps light in a corridor before releasing it into the interior. The approach has a distinct beauty, not unlike a Noh stage, and the ground elevates you ever so slightly, your feet almost floating above the ground. When you set foot in Inagawa Cemetery, you step onto a threshold from one world to the next—a stopping point which scrapes the heavens, lifting you onto another plane.

⁎

Right in front of the entrance is a staircase which bisects the terraces in a straight line, a bit like the steps on Teotihuacan's Pyramid of the Sun. It is an aesthetic with a sense of cosmic wonder. You begin to think that, just maybe, there is some hidden, mystical astronomy at work, defining every angle and contour. You feel like a beam of light might magically radiate out of the shrine at the top of the stairs, illuminating a singular point on the chapel wall at a singular moment in time—the same hour of the same day of the same month of every year, all the product of an ancient equation. An illusory summit lies in wait at the top, seemingly within reach but never attainable, a pursuit both Kafkaesque in its contradictions and like a Zen kōan in its mystery. Without that passage, at once emanating possibility and impossibility, the cemetery would lack vital elements: the opportunity for free imagination and an ethical

丘陵や山肌を利用した傾斜状の建築物に、静かな昂揚を感じる。地形と一体化しつつも、自然のなかに埋没するのではなく、幾何学の美しさで、逆に自然のうちに隠された数理の奇跡を引き出すような外観に私は惹かれるのだ。そういう場所に身を置いたら、下から上を見あげるのと、上から下を見おろすのと、どちらをより好ましく感じるのか、つい自問したくなる。

⚹

猪名川霊園の礼拝堂は、兵庫県北摂山系の急斜面に設けられた、シーランチのコンドミニアムのような、片流れの屋根を持つ見えない海に面した墓地の要である。傾斜地の墓地なら、いくつか足を踏み入れたことがある。たとえばパリのペール・ラシェーズ。あの墓地の幾何学には存分に計算された無秩序があった。人工の土地区画のなかに植えられた樹木が自然の姿をまとって散策路に覆いかぶさり、深い影と静寂をもたらす。気の流れはなにものにも妨げられない。沈黙だけが支配するのではなく死者との対話があり、質問に対する答えが用意されている。ただし空間を統御する管理棟は、味気ない郊外の一戸建ての風貌で、土地と合一しているとは思えない。

⚹

しかし猪名川霊園には、問いしかない。死者をして語らしめる無理強いがないのだ。鈴木理策が四季を通して捉えた世界には、残された者が問いを投げるだけで、回答を期待しない空気がただよっている。むしろ回答が還ってこないことによって深まる問いに満ちていると言ったほうがいいだろうか。もとより霊園は特定の死者のためのものだが、この空間に想像の身を委ねて感じられるのは、共同墓地に近い無名性の匂いだ。わたしの、あなたの、父の、母の、夫の、妻の、息子の、娘の、という所有格を尊重しながら、あえてそれをはぎ取った純粋形態の死。デイヴィッド・チッパーフィールドは、この墓地を「設計」したのではない。 すでにそこに積み重ねられてきたいくつもの死に敬意を払い、まるで火山灰から掘り出されたポンペイの遺跡のように、無傷でそこに遺されていたにぎわしい日常の死を、ただ誠実に「再生」しようとしただけである。無名性と無味乾燥が、匿名性と冷徹さがかならずしも結びつかないことを、この建築家はよく理解している。

⚹

閉鎖と開放が巧みに組み合わされ、ロマネスク教会のシンプルさと、白色を避けて赤土のように塗られた古い木造建築を思わせる意匠が、光をいったん回廊で包んでから内部へ送り込む。アプローチの美しさは能舞台のようでもあって、ここを通る者の足裏は、地面から少し浮いている。猪名川霊園は、私たちの生きるこの世界から、べつの世界へと足を踏み出すための、高所に位置する中継地なのである。

⚹

openness, a welcoming, unprejudiced environment for the deceased of any religious background or tradition. Some return to the earth. Some ascend into the heavens. Some vanish into the air. Inagawa Cemetery leaves every passage into the next world open.

The structures use light to full effect, too. Embracing the semi-darkness filling the space as an element to cherish, not banish, the design engenders an ambience sacred yet never oppressively sombre. A cemetery might be a stopping point for the soul on its journey from the here to the hereafter, but Inagawa Cemetery does not let that transitory nature downplay the relief of eternal rest. The architect's design captures the vitality of the distant past, far removed from the world we know, and somehow liberates that energy to resonate through the visitor lounge and fill the chapel. The water-transporting rill does not just add an aural touch; it is a spiritual conduit from the present life to the afterlife. With mediums for union shaping the entire space, the living and the dead can communicate in voiceless voices, the grieving and the grieved can meet on an equal standing, direct in their connection. God or no god, Buddha or no Buddha, it does not matter—the space conveys a sacredness, giving the cemetery all it needs. Inagawa Cemetery emanates that quality in every facet of its design. The courtyard behind a framed opening, invoking images of the Sanzu River and Lethe, brings the surrounding mountain nature into clearer, narrower focus, an environment which animates the imagination to extraordinary effect. The architects envisioned the courtyard as a place where visitors would enter a different sort of realm and imagine sprawling outer worlds in a smaller, more intimate setting. You get that sense when you are there. With the mountains in the distance forming a borrowed backdrop, the courtyard dissolves the boundaries separating your inner, emotional landscape from the visual world around you, creating a seamless whole. From their homes within the earth, the dead can hear the voices of their fellow deceased, find repose in oneness, foresee seeds turning into sprouts and stems and flowers and trunks and trees. They can imagine a larger world on scales both spatial and linear. Their imaginations stir while their bodies rest, filling the serenity of the place with a dynamic quality—not just stillness.

Inagawa Cemetery embodies a sacredness in the animistic sense: its structure embraces the variability of the seasons, while light and shadow breathe freely. In a way, it seems to have something 'Japanese'

エントランスの真正面に、ひな壇を貫いて一直線にあがっていく、テオティワカン遺跡の《太陽のピラミッド》を思わせる階段がある。もしかすると、ここには私たちのだれも知らない天文学の知見が秘められていて、毎年、ある月のある時刻に、階段の頂にある納骨堂から太陽光がまっすぐに伸びてきて、礼拝堂の特定の部分に当たるのかもしれない。目視できてもたどり着くことができないカフカ的な、あるいは禅の公案のような頂。可能性と不可能性をともに感じられるこの通路がなければ、偏見なく宗派も問わずに死者を迎え入れるという、健全な想像力と倫理に支えられた墓地は成立しない。土に還る。天に昇る。大気中に消え去る。どのような消え方も、ここでは許容されるだろう。

施設全体にただよっている幽冥の気配と、薄暗さを否定的なものにしない光の扱いには、まちがいなく聖性が感じられる。ただし、重苦しくはない聖性が。霊園を、この世からべつの世界へと移動する際の魂の中継地だと見なしたとしても、永眠の安堵感は喪われはしない。建築家は、私たちの知らない遠い過去のにぎわいを封じ込め、なにかのきっかけでそれが休憩室に、礼拝堂に響き伝えられる仕組みをつくっている。水を導く暗渠は音を伝えるだけではなく、冥界とこちらをつなぐ魂の導管でもある。声にならない声でのコミュニケーションが成立し、弔う者と弔われる者が、ほとんど等価になる。神がいてもいなくても、仏がいてもいなくても、空間の聖性が引き出されさえすれば、それでいい。三途の川にも、忘却の川にも通じる魂の閘門のなかに設けられた内庭は、周囲の山の自然を箱庭的に取り込む想像力の母体だ。建築家みずからが語っているように、訪れた者たちはその緑の内側に入り込んで、極小の景色から広大な外の世界を夢見る。周囲の山々の借景を利用することで自分の内側の光景と外側の光景を区別せず、ひとつづきにできるのだ。世界の内側に入って、死者は自分以外の死者たちの声を聴き、心を鎮め、一粒の種のなかに将来の芽や茎や花や幹の姿を見通すように、もっと大きな世界を見る。休息のなかで発動するそうした想像力こそが、ダイナミックな平穏さを生み出すのである。

四季の移り変わりをたくみに取り込んだ構造、光と影の呼吸、アニミズム的な意味における聖性。たしかに猪名川霊園には、「日本的」な気配がある。しかし幸運なことに、「日本的」という言い方でごまかされる薄っぺらな仕掛けはない。特定の神や仏よりも、ひとりの人間の顔を、彼を支えたひとつ前の世代の人々を、さらにまたひとつ前の世代から時間の位置エネルギーによってわき水を汲みあげ、それを再利用する魂の活性化があって、ひな壇ごとに整理整頓された印象は薄い。墓石の下に眠る者たちは、与えられた区画にけっして狭苦しさを感じないだろう。死してなお生きつづける彼らの想像力は、死後の理想よりも、宇宙的な無限を見ることに用いられる。

---

about it — but, fortunately, it is not the brand of 'Japaneseness' which serves as a convenient label for superficial qualities. The place is a font of spiritual revitalisation on a deeper level, drawing not on the salvation of a single god or Buddha but rather the formative flow propelling every individual into existence and through life. It taps a timeless torrent of potential energy, extending back from one generation to the next, all the way into the wellsprings of the immemorial. That process is primal, natural, and the cemetery reflects that in its aversion to meticulous arrangements — spatial perfection is not the point. Under their gravestones, the dead rest in comfort, not boxed-off, restrictive plots. They are free to keep imagining on a boundless scope. Instead of simply inhabiting the realm of some ideal for the afterlife, their imaginations can drift across a cosmic infinity.

I imagine myself at the top of the slope, gazing down at the gravestones below, all situated at comfortable distances from one another. I might have a lofty perspective, but I do not feel like some kind of all-powerful authority in command of some domain. I am struck with the magnitude of the moment. It is a sense of awe, fear laid bare, which overcomes me as I stand living above the dead. I then imagine myself at the bottom of the slope, staring up at the stepped walls. I move forward one step at a time, my coming journey immeasurable, my destination unseen, my faith planted in the belief that something lies at the top.

Inagawa Cemetery makes you perceive the experience in the context of up-and-down movement. It pulls you into a constant flux where the lines between life and death blur. Am I alive? Am I dead? Does it even matter? Nothing seems certain, and I could not care less. Free of any artificial contrast, free of any spiritual barriers, the space beckons me to rise, to fall, to traverse the realms of time and space. There is no fixed path, nothing locking me into a set route or stopping me from straying off course. I think I could plop myself down in the middle of the central staircase or find a spot on the gentle slant of a roof. I want to just stay there as long as I can, taking comfort in the surroundings. It is surprising, really. I am not even the slightest bit worried that I might end up here forever. The shock of that moment does not come from an encounter with death. Inagawa Cemetery does not inspire that sensation. To me, it is proof of a more vital life, new and fresh and vibrant.

想像のなかで、私は斜面のいちばん上に身を置き、密集から逃れて適度な間隔を置いた墓石の列を眺めおろす。下界のすべてを支配していることに満足した最高権力者の気分になったりはしない。むしろこれらの死者の上に立つことに対する畏怖と怯えをあらわにするだろう。また、想像のなかで、私は斜面のいちばん下に身を置き、段々の壁面を見あげる。どこまでのぼるのかわからないまま、その見えない頂にあるなにかを信頼して、まずは一段ずつ歩を進めていくだろう。

⁎

霊園に入った者には、かならずこの上下運動が課される。このとき、私たちは生きているのか、死んでいるのか。ある意味で、そんなことはどうでもいいと思えてくる。人工の明暗を抜け、魂の解放された空間をのぼりおりして、その運動を時空にも課す。迷子になりたくてもなれない明確な動線を最後までたどるかわりに、中央の階段の真ん中あたりに、あるいは心地よく傾斜した屋根の上に腰をおろして、もっとながくここにとどまっていたいと願う。このまま帰れなくなるかもしれないという不安を少しも感じないことに、私は驚く。そして、その驚きを死ではなくより新鮮な生の証として、深く受け止めることになるのだ。

Autumn 秋

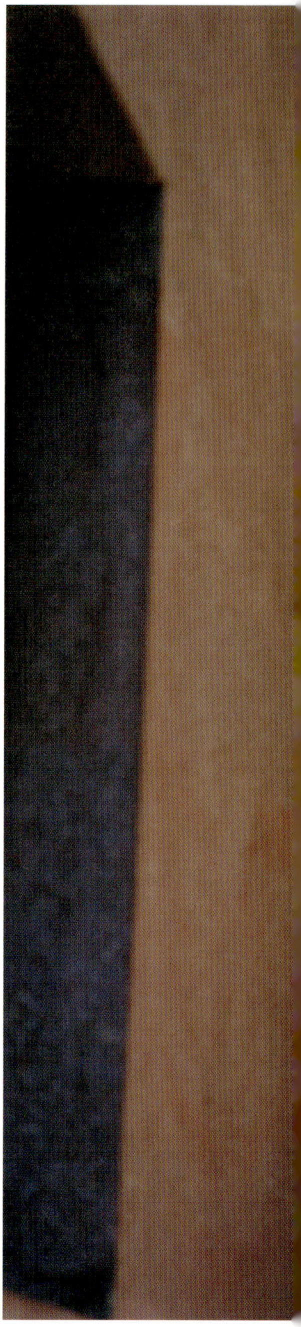

An awareness of the passage of time

時の移ろいへの気づき

Marcia Iwatate

岩立マーシャ

In joy or sadness, flowers are our constant friends.
Tenshin (Kakuzo) Okakura

'The garden is the heart of the building. Just as the cemetery is surrounded by trees, the garden becomes the nucleus of the place.' David Chipperfield's concept was the starting point of the landscape design. His architectural plan was pure and extremely clear—a large sloping roof responding to the gradient of the surrounding mountains and all building elements constructed with a single material, earth-like red coloured cast concrete. The coloured concrete resonates with the retaining stone walls, aged by the cemetery's 40-year history, continuing throughout the grounds.

I imagined the cloister garden (wildflower garden) to blend into the natural surroundings of Inagawa, taking inspiration from palettes and textures of Japanese meadows and woodlands, and seasonal icons used in haiku poetry. 67 species of native wildflowers, grasses and deciduous and evergreen shrubs were selected for their flowering seasons, autumn foliage, dried silhouettes and bare profiles. They are carefully calibrated to produce a gradually shifting polyphony throughout the seasons. The water channel garden, bordering the perimeters of the rill located in the middle of the staircase, is planted with wildflowers that thrive in full sun.

In contrast to the textural and vivid wildflower and water channel gardens, the grove of trees in the courtyard of the chapel features a serene garden harmonising with reflection and prayer. Taking the visitors' seated perspective into account, deciduous *Aodamo* trees (fraxinus lanuginosa f. serrata) with grey mottled trunks are selected for visual interest. Indigenous to the surrounding forests, the *Aodamo* tree is a hardy, slow-growing hardwood with a long-life expectancy. With feathery white spring blossoms, lime green summer foliage, burgundy autumn foliage and expressive winter trunks, it provides chapel visitors with an awareness of the seasons. A backdrop of evergreen *Hai no ki* (symplocaceae) saplings are planted to highlight the *Aodamo*'s bark and create a sense of depth. Ground cover is *Kamoji goke* moss (dicranum scoparium), *Inomoto so* ferns (pteris multifida), and *Hime nirinso* (anemone flaccida) producing a carpet of white blossoms in early spring.

I hope that the different expressions of the gardens throughout the seasons will provide visitors with an awareness of the passage of time; and the subtle transitions in the chapel garden gently embrace mourners as they bid farewell to their loved ones.

「喜びにつけ悲しみにつけ、花は不断の友である。」（岡倉天心）

「庭園はこの建築の中心であり、木々に囲まれた霊園の核を成すものである」。デイヴィッド・チッパーフィールドが提案したこのコンセプトは、ランドスケープ・デザインを考える出発点となった。礼拝堂と休憩棟の設計プランは、「敷地を囲む北摂山系の山々の急勾配に呼応する大きな片流れの屋根をもつ、単一の素材、赤土色に着色したコンクリートで造られた建築」というシンプルで明快なものだった。霊園自体は40年前からそこにあったもので、計画された建築の赤土色のコンクリートは、長い歳月がもたらした、霊園のひな壇の石垣の色彩と見事に調和していた。

チッパーフィールドの語る庭園のコンセプトと、建物の形状と色彩が自然と調和する環境を考えたとき、導き出されたのは、猪名川の自然を象徴しながら、その自然に溶け込むような中庭だった。《山野草の庭》は、野生の植物のなかから精選した67種の草花や低木で構成されている。日本の草原や森ならではのそれぞれの質感や色合い、そして俳句の季語などからも着想を得て、草花の開花時期や姿形、落葉樹の花季、黄葉・紅葉や落葉後の樹形と常緑樹の精気に満ちた姿や、四季の移り変わりから生成されるポリフォニーの調和を考えながら、それぞれを慎重に配置した。

彩り豊かな《山野草の庭》とは対照的に、礼拝堂の《樹々の庭》は故人を偲び、その想いを振り返り、祈りをささげる静謐な場として計画した。参拝者が着席したとき、少し低い目線の先に映るのは、幹に豊かな表情をもつ猪名川の森に自生する青梻（アオダモ）の木。成長が遅く寿命も長いこの樹木は、春には淡雪のような小さな花を咲かせ、夏には爽やかな緑の葉を蓄える。秋には鮮やかに紅葉し、冬には幹に白い模様を浮き立たせる。表情豊かなこの青梻の幹の風情を際立たせ、庭に奥行きが生まれるように、背景には常緑樹の灰の木（ハイノキ）を置き、足元は髢文字苔（カモジゴケ）と井口辺草（イノモトソウ）、姫二輪草（ヒメニリンソウ）の群生で覆った。春先には、木々の足下に二輪草の白い小さな花の絨毯が現れる。

山の斜面を流れる水路を草花で覆う《水路の庭》と、三つの庭の四季折々にみせる様々な庭の表情は、霊園を訪れたひとびとに移りゆく季節や悠然とした時間の流れをおおらかに伝え、礼拝堂から眺める庭の繊細な変化は、静かに祈りをささげるひとびとに親密さや慰めを与えるだろう。

Late May to mid-July

Yama ajisai Hydrangea serrata
(Mountain Hydrangea)

山紫陽花［ヤマアジサイ］

Native to Japan, the striking blue blossoms further enhanced by raindrops, brighten the gloomy rainy season weather. *Ajisai* is representative of Japanese flora along with *Sakura* (cherry blossom). Its name means 'a gathering of indigo'. *Ajisai* blooms come in many different colours and shapes, and various other names such as Seven Transformations, Eight Immortals Flower, and Snowball Flower exist. One of its binomial names was given by German physician and botanist Philipp Franz Balthasar von Siebold, who was posted to the Nagasaki Dutch Trading House in 1823. He named the largest and most beautiful blossoms *Otakusa* after his beloved mistress Taki Kusumoto (also known as Otaki-san). Countless *haiku* poems express the beauty of *Ajisai*. One poem reads, 'Hydrangea—light blue in hemp *kimono*' (Matsuo Basho).

梅雨時の雨に濡れてひときわ鮮やかに青色がさえる日本原産の紫陽花。由来は集と真藍が変化したもので、集は集まる、真藍は青い花という意味。多彩な色の変化から七変化や八仙花、丸く集まった姿から手毬花などとも呼ばれる。学名のひとつであるオタクサは幕末に長崎オランダ商館に来たドイツ人医師、植物学者でもあったシーボルトが最も大輪で美しい品種に、自分が愛した遊女、楠本滝（お滝さん）の名前を取って命名した。紫陽花の美しさは多くの俳人にしばしば詠まれている。「紫陽花や帷子時の薄浅黄」(松尾芭蕉)。

Early June to late July

Kikyo Platycodon grandifloras
(Balloon flower)

桔梗［キキョウ］

One of the Seven Flowers of Autumn (refer to *Ito susuki*, overleaf). Originally an icon to express autumn, it was classified as an endangered species, and new specimens were cultivated to bloom in the summer. As its name means 'good fortune', it was a popular motif for family crests and flag emblems during the civil wars of the Sengoku period (1467–1615).

秋の七草のひとつ。絶滅危惧種に指定され、最近では花季が長い園芸品種しか見られない。桔梗の字が「更に吉（さらによし）」の組み合わせになっていることから縁起がよいとされ、戦国時代には紋所や旗印として人気を集めた。「きりきりしやんとしてさく桔梗かな」（小林一茶）など多くの俳句も残っている。

Early June to late August

Utsubo gusa Prunella vulgaris
L subsp. asiatica

靫草［ウツボグサ］

The name traces back to the quivers in which samurai warriors stored their arrows. Its dried spikes are collected in the summer and brewed as 'heal-all' herbal medicine. Medicinal properties of subspecies have also been recognised in Western countries.

武士が弓を入れる矢筒の靫に由来する。夏に枯れた花穂は夏枯草（カゴソウ）と呼ばれ生薬として使われる。西洋でも靫草の亜種がメディカルハーブとして用いられるため、花言葉には「協調性」のほかに「優しく癒やす」という言葉も。

Early June to early September

Waremoko Sanguisorba officinalis (Great burnet)
吾亦紅［ワレモコウ］

An alternative name comes from a hat worn on the forehead in the Heian period (794–1185), reminiscent of the shape of its bottlebrush flowers. Although commonly thought of as an autumn flower, it has a long flowering period and was photographed in mid-summer for this publication. Its floriography 'transition' refers to the buds beginning to colour and bloom in succession from top to bottom.

「割れ木爪（帽額）」とも。この和名は、平安時代に額にかぶった帽額（もこう）から名付けられた。芒とともに十五夜の月見に欠かせない花季が長い秋の花。花言葉「移ろい」は、上から順に色づき咲いていく様子に由来する。止血などに使う薬草でもある。

Late June to early July

Kugai so Veronicastrum sibiricum (Culver's root)
九蓋草、九階草［クガイソウ］

This lilac, salverform herbaceous wildflower is native to sunny slopes in the highlands of Honshu Island. Its name means 'nine steps' from its leaf structure with horizontal whorls of four to eight leaves in nine steps.

本州に広く分布し、山地や高原の日当たりのよい草地に生育。名の由来は葉のつき方から来る。4枚から8枚の葉が輪生し、9層のおおいという意味の九蓋草と呼ばれるようになった。春先の若芽は食用にもなる。

Late July to early September

Miso hagi Lythraceae
禊萩［ミソハギ］

The etymology of its name refers to 'ablution' and *Miso hagi* is commonly used as an offering to the Buddhist altar or grave. As it blooms in August, a time in Japanese tradition of welcoming back ancestors' spirits and returning to one's family roots, it reminds one of paying respect to loved ones who have passed away.

禊萩はお墓や仏前への供え花のひとつで、字の示すとおり様々な禊ぎの儀式にも使われる。お盆の頃に咲く姿を見て、亡くなった方に思いをはせることから、「愛の悲しみ」という花言葉がつけられた。

Late July to mid-September

Nori utsugi Hydrangea paniculata
糊空木［ノリウツギ］

The name refers to the tube-like hollow in its branch when the pith is removed, and to its sap, used as a paste-like medium for floating bush fibres to produce *washi* paper. With gorgeous clusters of white blossoms, it is a member of the hydrangea family that blooms later than other species under the hot summer sun. It is hardy and highly adaptable.

小さな白い花の集まる様子が愛らしい糊空木は、枝の髄を抜くと空洞ができること、また樹液を糊として和紙を漉くときに使ったことからその名がついた。紫陽花の仲間だが、紫陽花に遅れ真夏に盛りを迎える。

Late July to late September

Fushiguro senno Silene miqueliana
節黒仙翁［フシグロセンノウ］

An endemic species to Japan. Its vermillion colour is exceptional among Japanese wildflowers, and it was used as *chabana* (flowers suiting the tea ceremony aesthetic) and *rikka* (Buddhist style of arrangement placed upright in a copper vase) since ancient times. Its name refers to the black stem joints and to the Senno-ji Temple in Kyoto, where it was first discovered.

日本の固有種。山野草のなかでもひときわ色鮮やかな朱色花弁をつける節黒仙翁は、古くから茶花や立花に用いられた。その美しさと似つかぬ花の名は、茎の節の部分が黒褐色であることと、京都・嵯峨の仙翁寺で発見されたことに由来する。

Late July to early October

Ominaeshi Veronicastrum sibiricum
女郎花［オミナエシ］

Its name means beauty overwhelming a beautiful woman. It is mentioned in the 11th century novel *The Tales of Genji* depicting the lifestyle of Heian courtiers, as a garden flower and expressing colour combinations in the elaborate layering of court *kimono*.

古語「をみな」は若く美しい女性、「えし」は「へし（圧）」を示し、美女を圧倒する花の美しさから名づけられた。『源氏物語』でも和歌に詠まれるだけでなく、前栽の花や襲（かさね）の色目の名として登場する。

Late August to October

Ito susuki Miscanthus sinensis f. gracillimus (Japanese silver grass)
糸芒［イトススキ］

'Flowers blossoming in autumn fields, when I count them on my fingers, they number seven.' (Yamanoue no Okura). As this verse suggests, *Susuki* is one of the Seven Flowers of Autumn beloved in Japan for centuries. Essential for the full-moon banquet setting alongside 'moon-viewing' rice cakes, autumn produce, and sake, which are offerings to the moon to pray for an abundant harvest. This celebration takes place on the 15th day of the eighth month of the traditional lunar calendar, in September or October of the modern solar calendar. This custom originated with aristocrats in the Heian-period (794–1185) who gathered to celebrate and recite poetry under the full moon. The Seven Flowers of Autumn include *Susuki*, *Kikyo* (previous spread), and *Ominaeshi* (opposite), along with *Hagi* (bush clover), *Kuzu* (arrowroot), *Nadeshiko* (dianthus), and *Fuji bakama* (joe-pye weed).

「秋の野に咲きたる花を指折りかき数ふれば七種の花」（山上臣憶良）。山や草原に群生する芒は秋の風情を象徴する植物のひとつ。平安時代から続く明月を愛でる風習、十五夜の月見には欠かせない供物である。秋の七草とは本書にも登場する桔梗、吾亦紅、女郎花のほかに萩（ハギ）、葛（クズ）、撫子（ナデシコ）、藤袴（フジバカマ）。

Mid-October (autumn foliage)

Dodan tsutsuji Enkianthus perulatus
満天星躑躅［ドウダンツツジ］

Dodan tsutsuji is a compact, slow-growing deciduous shrub native to sunny woodlands of Japan. The etymology of its name refers to a 'sky full of stars', an image conjured by the tiny white blossoms covering the entire shrub in spring. The stunning scarlet red autumn foliage is calibrated to contrast with the silvery plumes of *Ito susuki*.

日当たりがよい森林に自生する低木。真っ白な花が株全体を覆う姿が、白々と星の輝く星空を連想させることから名づけられた。また、「どうだん」は灯台が転じたもので、枝分かれする様子が灯台の脚部と似ていることからその名がついたともいわれる。秋の草原をイメージし、真っ赤に紅葉する姿と銀色の糸芒の穂とのコントラストを考えた。

January to March

Kanzaki ayame Iris unguicularis
寒咲き菖蒲（カンザキアヤメ）

Unlike normal irises that drop their leaves in winter, this rare species is evergreen and blooms during the grim winter months when there is very little else that brings color to the garden. Nestled under long arching leaves, the deep violet flowers have beautiful white and yellow markings and a sweet scent.

通常のアヤメと異なり葉が枯れない常緑性の多年草。花のない冬の寒い時期に開花する珍種。濃い紫色の花びらの弁元にある、白と黄色の網目状の模様の美しさや甘い香りも魅力的である。

Late March to late April

Hime nirinso Anemone flaccida
姫二輪草［ヒメニリンソウ］

The name refers to the two flowers blooming atop each stem. Reminiscent of two close friends, its floriography is associated with 'friendship' and 'never parting'. In March, clusters of *Hime nirinso* produce a carpet of white blossoms in the grove of trees garden located in the chapel courtyard.

二輪草の名はひとつの茎から2輪の花を咲かせることに由来する。その様子が仲のよい友だちのようにみえることから、「友情」「ずっと離れない」という花言葉をもつ。3月、礼拝堂の《樹々の庭》には白いカーペットが広げられたような二輪草の群生がみられる。

Late March to May

Yamabuki Kerria japonica
山吹［ヤマブキ］

Yamabuki holds sentimental connotations of spring in the hearts of the Japanese. The origin of its name comes from its yellow blossoms wavering in the wind, appearing as though the entire mountain is trembling. An ancient myth depicts two lovers who, forced to separate, bury a mirror in the ground with their last reflections together before parting. The spot was quickly covered by flowering *Yamabuki* shrubs. It is also mentioned frequently in *The Tale of Genji.* One excerpt portrays the beauty of a princess as dew drops glowing in the sun when *Yamabuki* blossoms are in full bloom.

春の木の脇役として日本人の心を捉えてきた山吹。風になびく細い枝が山を振り動かしているような風情から「山振（やまぶり）」と名づけられ、後に訛り「山吹」となる。恋仲を裂かれた男女が別れ際に自分たちの面影を映した鏡を土に埋め、そこに山吹が生い茂ったという伝説がある。『源氏物語』にも繰り返し登場し、中将が姫君の美しさを「八重山吹が咲き乱れたる盛りに露かかれる夕映えぞ」と思い浮かべたりしている。

Illustrations by KISHICRI　イラスト：きしくり

Winter 冬

Appendix

資料

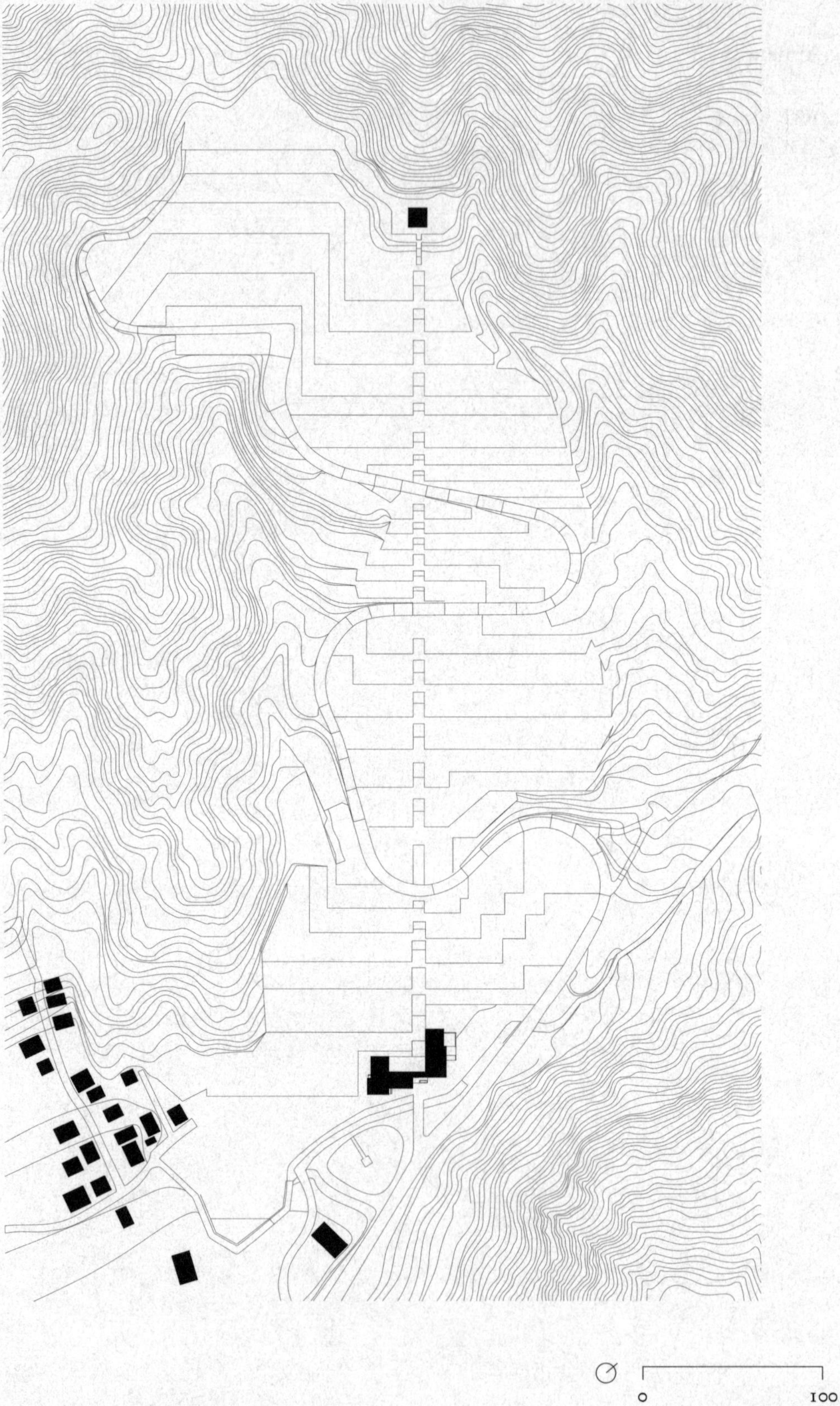
0
100

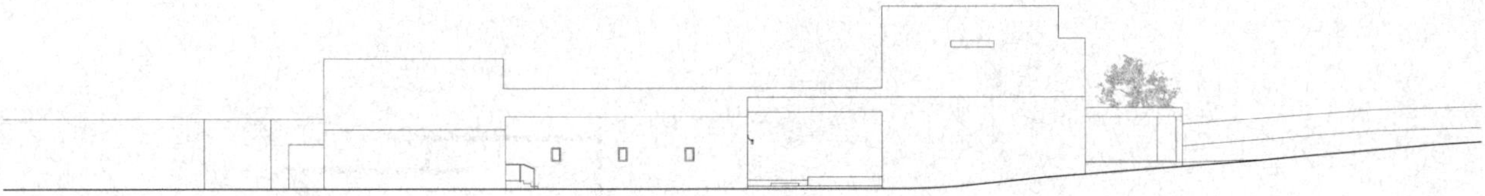

East

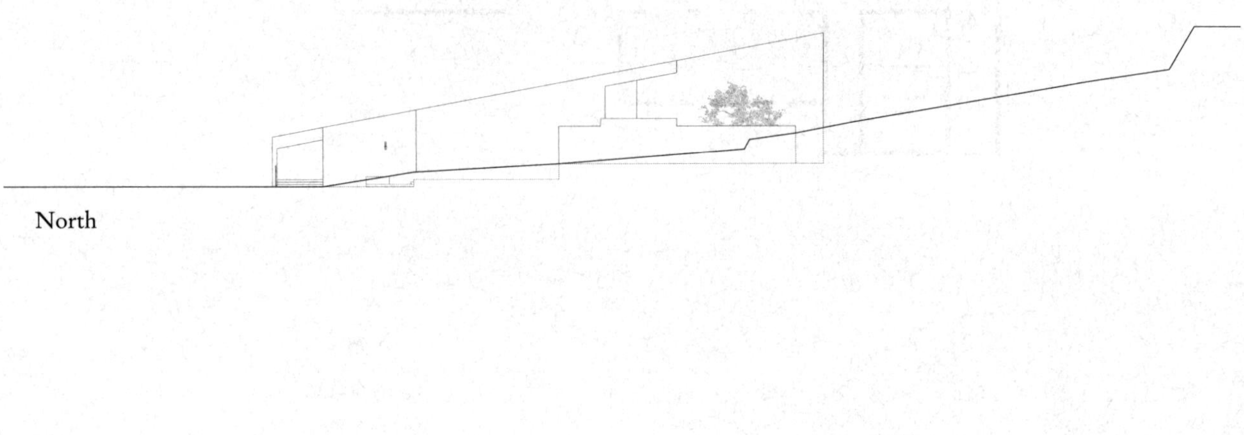

North

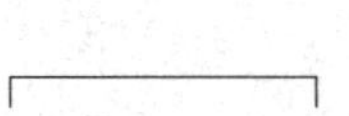

1 Entrance from car park
2 Chapel
3 Chapel gardens
4 Altar
5 Reception
6 Archive
7 Staff room
8 Staff changing room
9 Entrance
10 Memorial rooms
11 Lavatories
12 Visitors' room
13 Vending machines
14 Pantry
15 Plant area
16 Wildflower garden
17 Walkway
18 Stairs to cemetery
19 Water points

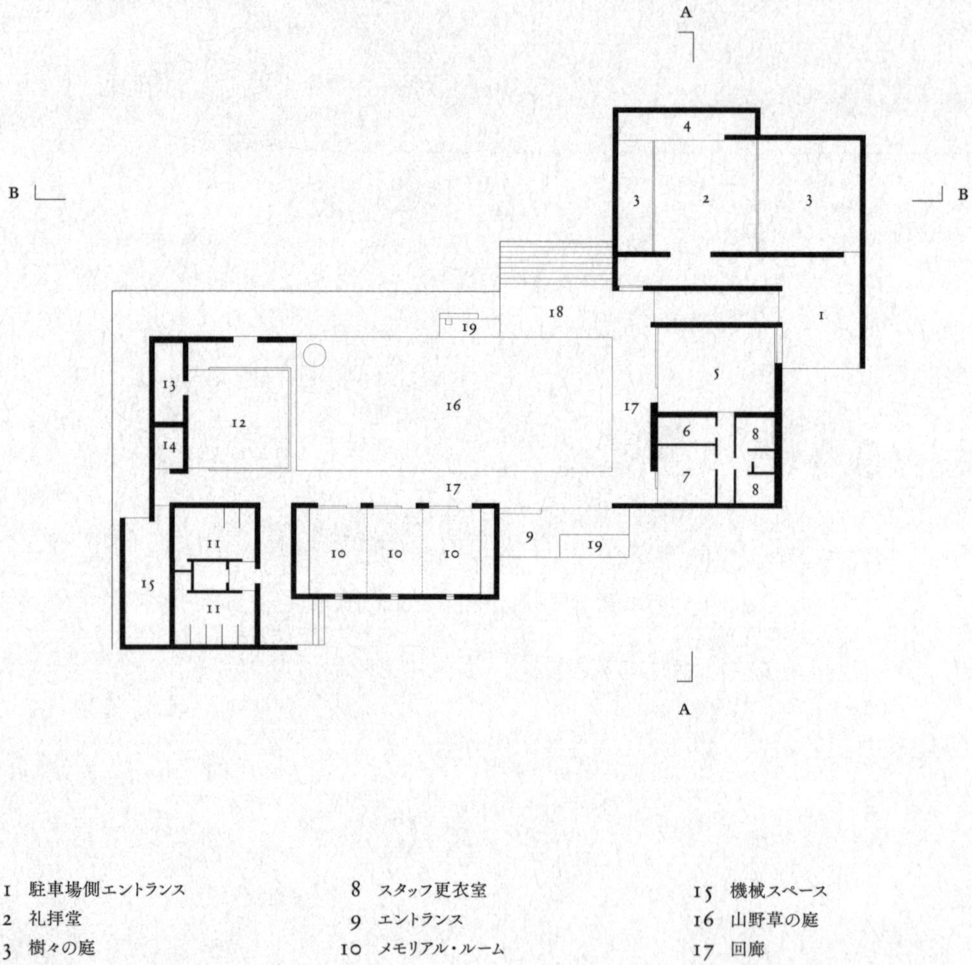

1 駐車場側エントランス
2 礼拝堂
3 樹々の庭
4 祭壇
5 レセプション
6 書庫
7 スタッフ・ルーム
8 スタッフ更衣室
9 エントランス
10 メモリアル・ルーム
11 トイレ
12 ビジター・ラウンジ
13 自動販売機
14 パントリー
15 機械スペース
16 山野草の庭
17 回廊
18 墓地への階段
19 水盤

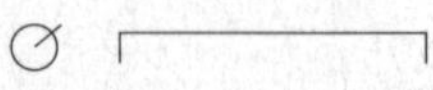

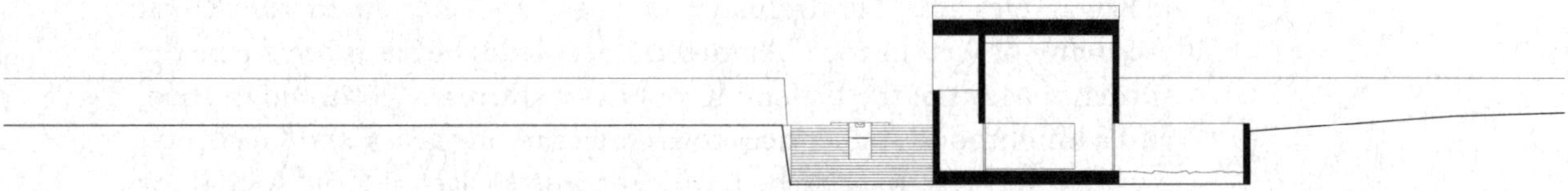

AA

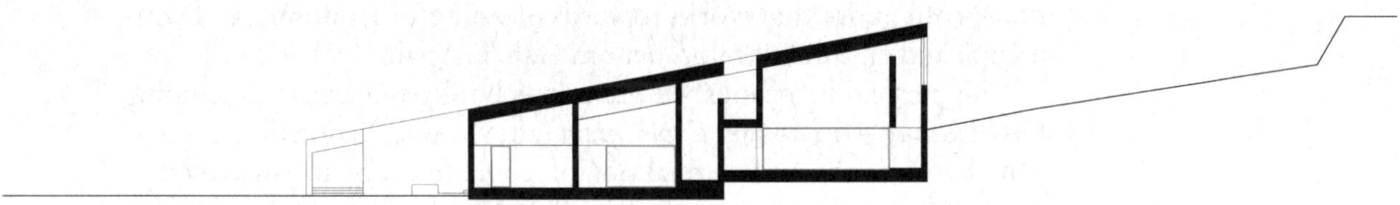

BB

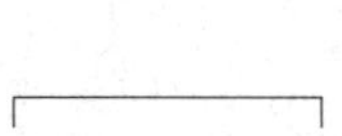

David Chipperfield, born in London in 1953, is an architect. He studied architecture at the Kingston School of Art and the Architectural Association School of Architecture in London before founding his own practice in 1985. He has built a design methodology that is now used across four offices in London, Berlin, Milan and Shanghai.

Chipperfield is a member of the Royal Institute of British Architects and an honorary fellow of both the American Institute of Architects and the Bund Deutscher Architekten. He was appointed Commander of the Order of the British Empire in 2004, appointed a Royal Designer for Industry in 2006, and elected to the Royal Academy of Arts in 2008. Among the accolades he has received are the Order of Merit of the Federal Republic of Germany, awarded in 2009, and a knighthood for services to architecture in the UK and Germany, awarded in 2010. In 2011 he received the RIBA Royal Gold Medal for Architecture, and in 2013, the Praemium Imperiale from the Japan Art Association, both given in recognition of a lifetime's work.

In addition to design work, Chipperfield has taught and lectured worldwide at schools of architecture in Austria, Italy, Switzerland, the United Kingdom and the United States. He holds honorary doctorates from Kingston University and the University of Kent. In 2012 he curated the 13th International Architecture Exhibition of the Venice Biennale under the title *Common Ground*. He served as the mentor for architecture from 2016–17 for the Rolex Mentor and Protégé Arts Initiative. In 2017 he founded Fundación RIA, a private, non-profit entity that works towards meaningful economic, environmental and cultural development in Galicia, Spain.

Chipperfield has published numerous books and articles, including *On Planning – A Thought Experiment* (2018), a publication that explores and theorises the urban qualities of contemporary urban developments. He was the 2020 guest editor of Italian design magazine *Domus.*

デイヴィッド・チッパーフィールド

建築家。1953年、ロンドン生まれ。ロンドンのキングストン芸術学校、AAスクール（英国建築協会付属建築学校）で建築を学び、85年、デイヴィッド・チッパーフィールド・アーキテクツを設立。築き上げた設計方法論は、ロンドン、ベルリン、ミラノ、上海にある4つのオフィスで実践されている。

王立英国建築家協会（RIBA）会員、米国建築家協会、ドイツ建築家連合名誉会員であり、2004年には大英帝国勲章（CBE）を受章、06年、王室工業デザイナー、08年、ロイヤル・アカデミー会員に選出される。ほかに、09年、ドイツ連邦共和国功労勲章、10年、ドイツと英国における建築への功績に対する下級勲爵士の称号など。また、これまでの生涯にわたる功績に対して、11年に王立英国建築家協会（RIBA）よりロイヤル・ゴールド・メダル、13年に日本美術協会より高松宮殿下記念世界文化賞が授与された。

チッパーフィールドは設計に加えて、オーストリア、イタリア、スイス、英国、米国など世界中の建築学校で教鞭を執り、講義を行ってきた。イギリスのキングストン大学とケント大学からは名誉博士号を与えられている。ほかに、12年、第13回ヴェネチア・ビエンナーレ国際建築展「Common Ground」キュレーター、16〜17年、ロレックス・アーツ・イニシアティブおよびプロテジェ・アーツ・イニシアティブでメンターを務める。17年には、スペインのガリシアで経済、環境、文化の有意義な発展に向けて活動する民間の非営利団体「Fundación RIA」を設立。

現代の都市開発における都市のありかたを探究し理論化した『On Planning—A Thought Experiment』（Walther König, 2018）をはじめ、著作も多数。20年、イタリアの建築雑誌『Domus』のゲスト編集を務めた。

Thomas Struth, born in 1954 in Geldern, Germany, and based in Berlin, is a photographer. He was part of the first generation of artists to study photography with Bernd and Hilla Becher. Solo exhibitions of Struth's work have been presented at institutions including the Stedelijk Museum (Amsterdam), The National Museum of Modern Art (Tokyo), The Metropolitan Museum of Art (New York), the Museo Nacional del Prado (Madrid), the Museum Folkwang (Essen) and the Haus der Kunst (Munich). Struth was awarded the Spectrum International Prize for Photography by Kulturstiftung Lower Saxony in 1997. He is Honorary Fellow of The Royal Photographic Society of Great Britain and Foreign Honorary Member of the American Academy of Arts and Letters.

Hideyuki Osawa, born in Tokyo in 1957, is the president of the Boenfukyukai Foundation. As the head of the organisation, Osawa oversees the operations of five cemeteries across Japan. He has also served in a variety of other leadership positions, including executive director of the All Japan Cemetery Association. Modern art is another passion for Osawa. In addition to accumulating an extensive collection of pieces, he has held positions at prestigious institutions, such as The Metropolitan Museum of Art (New York), The Tate (London), and The Royal Academy of Arts (London), and built an international network of connections in the art world.

Toshiyuki Horie, born in Gifu in 1964 and currently based in Tokyo, is a writer and scholar of Japanese literature. Horie's essays on his experiences studying in France began to appear in *Fransu* [France] in 1994, and *Kōgai he* [To the Suburbs], a collection of the pieces in book form, in 1995. He would go on to win the Mishima Yukio Prize for *Oparaban* [*Auparavant*] (1999) and the Akutagawa Prize for *The Bear and the Paving Stone* (2001). In the years since, Horie has won an array of different literary prizes in Japan. *The Bear and the Paving Stone* and several other entries in his oeuvre have been translated into English and French.

Risaku Suzuki, born in Shingū, Wakayama, Japan, and based in Tokyo, is a photographer. Fascinated by the dynamics of the gaze and the mediality of photography, Suzuki has embraced his creative energies in photographing a diverse array of subjects: the Kumano region, where he grew up; the natural phenomena and landscapes of snow, cherry trees, and water reflections; Montagne Sainte-Victoire, the mountain range in Southern France that inspired numerous works by Cézanne; and Cézanne's personal studio. In addition to publishing *Piles of Time* (2000), which won the 25th Kimura Ihei Award, Suzuki has also held multiple solo exhibitions in Japan and abroad.

Marcia Iwatate, born in Washington, D.C., and based in Tokyo, is the principal of Marcia Iwatate Office. After a career in fashion advertising, Iwatate has worked on wide-ranging consulting and creative direction for restaurant projects and new brand development. Her extensive list of projects abroad recently includes restaurants and cafés and at JW Marriott Hotel Seoul. Iwatate has also written numerous books on Japanese and Korean architecture, design, and cuisine for Western audiences. Iwatate's work on the landscape design for Inagawa Cemetery was a collaborative effort with Junya Kamimura (Kamimura Landscape Architects).

KISHICRI, born and based in Tokyo, is an artist and illustrator. From magazines and album designs to commercials and installations, KISHICRI's creative output covers a broad palette that even includes three-dimensional art, characters, tour merchandise, and tableware stylings. Recent projects include a wall painting for a *teppanyaki* eatery (Kurosawa) and a ceiling painting for a well-established bar (Monde Bar Hasegawa).

トーマス・シュトルート

写真家。1954年、ドイツ、ゲルダーン生まれ、ベルリンにて活動。ベルント&ヒラ・ベッヒャー夫妻に薫陶を受けたベッヒャー派の第一世代のひとり。アムステルダム市立近代美術館、東京国立近代美術館、メトロポリタン美術館(ニューヨーク)、プラド美術館(マドリード)、フォルクヴァング美術館(エッセン)、ハウス・デア・クンスト(ミュンヘン)などで個展を開催。97年ニーダーザクセン基金よりスペクトラム国際写真賞を受賞。英国王立写真協会名誉フェロー、アメリカ芸術文学アカデミー外国人名誉会員。

大澤秀行(おおさわ・ひでゆき)

公益財団法人墓園普及会理事長。1957年、東京生まれ。同会理事長として全国5霊園の墓地供給・管理事業を営み、公益社団法人全日本墓園協会常任理事などを歴任。また、現代美術作品のコレクターとしても知られ、メトロポリタン美術館(ニューヨーク)、テート(ロンドン)、ロイヤル・アカデミー・オブ・アーツ(ロンドン)をはじめ海外の美術館で様々な役職を務め、芸術分野での国際的な交流を行っている。

堀江敏幸(ほりえ・としゆき)

小説家、文学者。1964年、岐阜生まれ、東京にて活動。1994年より雑誌『ふらんす』にてフランス留学時の経験を綴った連載を開始、翌95年『郊外へ』として初の単行本化。99年『おぱらばん』で三島由紀夫賞、2001年「熊の敷石」で芥川龍之介賞、03年「スタンス・ドット」で川端康成文学賞、04年、同作収録の『雪沼とその周辺』で谷崎潤一郎賞、木山捷平文学賞、06年『河岸忘日抄』、10年『正弦曲線』で読売文学賞、12年『なずな』で伊藤整文学賞、16年『その姿の消し方』で野間文芸賞ほか、受賞多数。

鈴木理策(すずき・りさく)

写真家。1963年、和歌山県新宮市生まれ、東京にて活動。見ることへの問いと写真のもつメディア性への関心から、生地である熊野や、雪、桜、水鏡などの事象や風景、画家セザンヌが繰り返し描いた南仏のサント=ヴィクトワール山やセザンヌのアトリエを撮影した作品などを発表。2000年『Piles of Time』で第25回木村伊兵衛写真賞受賞。サンフランシスコ現代美術館、ヒューストン美術館、東京国立近代美術館、東京都写真美術館、国際交流基金などに作品が収蔵されている。

岩立マーシャ(いわたて・まーしゃ)

Marcia Iwatate Office主宰。米国ワシントンD.C.生まれ、東京にて活動。ファッション広告の仕事を経て、レストランおよび新規ブランドの総合プロデュースなどを手がける。近年の主な仕事にJWマリオット・ホテル・ソウル内のレストランやカフェをはじめ、海外でのプロジェクト多数。また、『春秋』(杉本貴志との共著、チャールズ・イ・タトル出版)をはじめ、欧米諸国に日本や韓国の建築、デザイン、料理を紹介する著書多数。猪名川霊園のランドスケープデザインは、上村純也(上村景観設計)と行った。

きしくり

アーティスト、イラストレーター。東京生まれ、同地にて活動。雑誌やCDジャケット、コマーシャルなどのイラストレーションをはじめ、立体オブジェやキャラクターデザイン、アーティストのツアーグッズ、食器のスタイリングなどを手がける。近作に、築地の鉄板焼「黒澤」のウォールペイント、銀座の老舗バー「MONDE BAR HASEGAWA」の天井画など。

Inagawa Cemetery Chapel and Visitor Centre
猪名川霊園　礼拝堂・休憩棟

Inagawa, Hyogo, Japan 2013–17
猪名川、兵庫　2013–17

Opening　オープニング
30 June 2017
2017年6月30日

Location　所在地
27 Shimizu Kitatani, Inagawa-cho,
Kawabe District, Hyogo Prefecture
兵庫県川辺郡猪名川町清水北谷27番地

Gross floor area　延床面積
500 m2

Client　建主
Boenfukyukai Foundation
公益財団法人墓園普及会

Architect　設計
David Chipperfield Architects
デイヴィッド チッパーフィールド アーキテクツ

Project director　プロジェクト ディレクター
David Chipperfield
デイヴィッド・チッパーフィールド

Project architects　プロジェクトアーキテクト
Matt Ball
マット・ボール
Tom Herre
トム・ヘーレ

Project team　プロジェクトチーム
Mira Abad　ミラ・アバド
Ricardo Alvarez　リカルド・アルヴァレス
Clemens Gerritzen　クレメンス・ゲルリッツェン
Amandine Kastler　アマンディーン・カストレル
Rik Nys　リック・ナイス
Patrick Ueberbacher　パトリック・ユーバーバッハー
Richard Youel　リチャード・ユーロ

Project manager　プロジェクトマネージャー
Naoko Kawamura
川村直子

Associate architect　アソシエイトアーキテクト
Akira Koyama　小山光
Akira Hanjo　繁昌朗
Key Operation Inc. /Architects
株式会社キー・オペレーション一級建築士事務所

Landscape architect
ランドスケープアーキテクト
Marcia Iwatate Office
and Kamimura Landscape Architects
岩立マーシャオフィス＋上村景観設計

Contractor and executive architect
実施設計・施工
Obayashi Corporation
株式会社大林組

Structural consultant
構造設計コンサルタント
Jun Sato Structural Engineering
佐藤淳構造設計事務所

Service consultant
設備設計コンサルタント
es associates
株式会社イーエスアソシエイツ

Lighting　照明
Viabizzuno Srl
ヴィアヴィッツーノSrl

Signage　サイン計画
Hayashi Takuma Design Office
林琢磨デザイン事務所

Textile　テキスタイル
NUNO Corporation
株式会社布

Furniture　家具
Cassina IXC. Ltd
株式会社カッシーナ・イクスシー

This book is co-published by LIXIL Publishing and Verlag der Buchandlung Walther und Franz König to present the concept of the Inagawa Cemetery Chapel and Visitor Centre that was completed in Hyogo Prefecture, Japan, in 2017.

Supervisor
Boenfukyukai Foundation

Design
John Morgan and Adrien Vasquez, John Morgan studio

Japanese typesetting
Tetsuya Goto

Editors
Cecilia Sundström and Olivia Lawrence Bright, David Chipperfield Architects
Chinatsu Kuma, LIXIL Publishing

Translators
Tetsuo Kinoshita, Tom Kain, Christopher Stephens, Sachie Watanabe

Print
Tosho Printing

Published by
Verlag der Buchhandlung Walther und Franz König
Ehrenstr. 4, D-50672 Köln

Bibliographic information published by the Deutsche Nationalbibliothek. The Deutsche Nationalbibliothek lists this publication in the Deutsche Nationalbibliografie; detailed bibliographic data are available at dnb.d-nb.de.

Printed in Japan

Vertrieb / Distribution

Europe
Buchhandlung Walther König
Ehrenstr. 4, D-50672 Köln
+49 (0) 221 / 20 59 6 53
verlag@buchhandlung-walther-koenig.de

UK & Ireland
Cornerhouse Publications Ltd.
2 Tony Wilson Place
UK – Manchester M15 4FN
+44 (0) 161 212 3466
publications@cornerhouse.org

Japan
LIXIL Publishing, LIXIL Corporation
2-1-1 Ojima Koto-ku
JAPAN – Tokyo 1360072
+81 (0) 3-3638-8021
xbn@lixil.com

Outside Europe and Japan
D.A.P. / Distributed Art Publishers, Inc.
75 Broad Street, Suite 630
USA – New York, NY 10004
+1 (0) 212 627 1999
orders@dapinc.com

ISBN 978-3-96098-890-8

Spring 春